Reading Tea Leaves
After Trump

Poetry & Prose by Award-Winning Author

Thelma T. Reyna

Golden
Foothills
PRESS

Copyright © 2018 by Thelma T. Reyna

Published by Golden Foothills Press
1443 E. Washington Boulevard, #232
Pasadena, CA 91104
www.GoldenFoothillsPress.com

Grateful acknowledgment is made to editors and publishers for permission to reprint poems previously published elsewhere. Credit for prior publication is provided in Acknowledgments section at the end of this book.

Library of Congress Cataloging-in-Publication Data
Reading Tea Leaves After Trump, by Thelma T. Reyna
--1st ed.
p. cm.

ISBN 978-0-9969632-3-7

1. Poetry and prose 2. Donald Trump 3. Presidential election 2016 4. Tea leaves 5. Poet Laureate 1. Reyna, Thelma T.

18 19 10 9 8 7 6 5 4 3 2 1

First Edition: 2018

Cover photo: "Woman covers her face with her hands, surreal concept, photo manipulation." Photo No. 248461363, adapted from www.shutterstock.com.
Author photo, back cover: Jesus Salvador Treviño
Book design: Thelma T. Reyna
Cover design: Thelma T. Reyna and Dom Gilormini
Printed in the United States of America

Advance Praise for
Reading Tea Leaves After Trump

This is a work of empathy in the best sense. Without apology, Reyna steps into the worlds of others and tries to feel her way into their pain, anger, and frustration, elusive as it might be. She animates Trump's base and reveals how their anguish and confusion were so easily mobilized by forces that didn't truly care about their well-being.

--Robin D.G. Kelley, Ph.D.
[From the Introduction]
Gary B. Nash Distinguished Professor
American History: UCLA

If poets are the prophets of our age, Thelma T. Reyna is not only a prophet but a first responder to the Trump era. Placing her poems like bandages over bleeding lies and broken promises, Reyna soothes the pain of a nation in crisis as only a gifted poet can: with clear truth, righteous anger, and deep empathy.

--Cassie Premo Steele, Ph.D.
National Award-Winning Poet
Author, *Tongues in Trees: Poems 1993-2017*

Stunning, heartfelt and deeply honest. Reyna presents to us the forecast of an unfolding aftermath and beyond. Here you have the full impact of today's political landscape in a powerful poetic voice with gems like "Crooked" so suitable for framing.

--Beverly M. Collins
Pushcart Prize in Poetry Nominee
Multiple Award-Winning Poet
Author, *Mud in Magic*

No voice is too small. Empathy is engendered for immigrants, victims, even the First Lady. Reyna's natural lyricism stitches tweets into a memorable pastiche of triplet verse, invokes details of political fray, and paints the mayhem that has daily hit and twisted a double-edged sword into our nation. The voices here are distinct, painfully recognizable and unforgettable.

--Carolyn Clark, Ph.D.
Writing Coach/Leader, The Writer's Center
Author, *New Found Land*

Reading Tea Leaves After Trump

Poetry & Prose by Award-Winning Author

Thelma T. Reyna

To the women, men, and children in America who have marched and protested to keep our nation's values— equality, democracy, social justice, and the peaceful well-being of ALL people—at the forefront of our nation's consciousness since November 2016.

Author's Foreword

I began writing this book in November, two weeks after the 2016 presidential election. I had followed the campaign closely, had watched each debate, and, like many, was stunned by the campaign's deviation from normalcy, due mostly to Donald J. Trump's behavior and rhetoric. The election result upended my hopes for history to be made with the election of our first woman president, Hillary Clinton.

For three days I grieved but couldn't weep. It took time for the dam to break, but tears for Trump's election were only the first of many reasons for feeling despair and some level of grief as weeks passed. From the outset, our nation's new president seemed intent on sowing disorder: attacking individuals and entire groups, vowing to dismantle institutions, policies, traditions our nation revered. Trump was, as many of his supporters agreed in polls, divisive, dishonest, and untrustworthy.

So how did he win the biggest leadership prize on earth? He became our first president with no governance or military experience. He claimed that his wealth and success as a businessman would enable him—and only him!—to solve the nation's problems, but each day of his campaign and his transition period belied this notion.

To understand what happened to America in November, and what was happening since, I read daily about Trump's agenda, his supporters and executive orders, advisors, behaviors, and words. I delved into our civic disruptions and hurtful spasms of division, read articles by bipartisan pundits, journalists, Pulitzer Prize winners, and academics as they parsed chaotic events and Trump's rhetoric, trying to make sense of what many termed the fraying of our nation's fabric.

Seeking catharsis, I explored in poetry and occasional prose the unfolding of troubling issues, expressed in envisioned voices of people affected by Trump. Reflecting *their* personas rather than simply my perspectives helped me view quandaries more meaningfully. This book's purpose showed itself: to help other flummoxed compatriots, to examine select political events or issues through different lenses, to provide solidarity in our nation's angst.

I also turned to *On Grief and Grieving: Finding the Meaning of Grief Through the Five Stages of Loss,** an iconic book by Elisabeth Kubler-Ross and David Kessler. I summarized Elisabeth's famous five stages—denial, anger, negotiating, depression, and acceptance—in a poem for each, which became the framework for this book.

This hybrid collection doesn't claim to be comprehensive. In a year battered by intense sociopolitical issues, and by unprecedented natural and manmade catastrophes, simply choosing what to write about felt like a Gordian task. Many convulsive events and uncivilities are absent here, but what appears are matters close to my heart, and perhaps to others' hearts, too.

Finally: the title of this book reflects the state of flux we live in under Trump. A tea leaf reader has as much of a shot at deciphering what Trump will do as insiders might. Also, it's a touch of whimsy, since the book holds no political expertise. I am merely a poet and storyteller, as inexpert at political understanding as a tea leaf reader.

Yet I hope that this book helps readers reflect on our society's issues, understand them a bit more, and facilitate recovery from a sense of loss. As divided as our nation currently is, at heart we're still all Americans desiring the best for our country.

—T.R.

---

* Elisabeth Kubler-Ross, MD, & David Kessler's *On Grief and Grieving: Finding the Meaning of Grief Through the Five Stages of Loss.* (Simon & Shuster, 2005). Kubler-Ross points out that the stages can occur out of sequence, be repeated cyclically with overlap, and some stages might be skipped.

Introduction

by Robin D.G. Kelley, Ph.D.

Gary B. Nash Distinguished Professor of American History
University of California, Los Angeles

Reading Tea Leaves After Trump is so much more than a collection of stirring poetic reactions to our surreal and dark times. I read it as a play in five acts. Like all great playwrights, Thelma T. Reyna is able to transform her *personal* grief into an expression of our *collective* grief. Each act moves us through the emotional stages of loss as we grieve the temporary death of democracy; the casualties of the latest war on the poor, on women, the black and brown, the vulnerable, the dispossessed; the snuffing out of reason and tolerance; the lethal body blows to Mother Earth. The curtain opens onto a state of disbelief and denial, like walking into our house after a burglary. Reyna finds voice(s) for her rage and ours, filling the stage with characters that help us navigate the new reality, fight depression, and come to terms with what we must do next.

And what characters! Melania, Hillary, Kellyanne Conway and her daughters, James Comey, the two deadly Steves (Bannon and Miller), Betsy De Vos, Martin Luther King, Jr., Heather Heyer, mothers and brothers, the dreadfully ill, the homeless, the undocumented, the Muslim, the fascist, the young soldier, the walking wounded, and of course, the Donald himself, take successive turns in the spotlight. Sets change: the White House, the halls of Congress, streets, the bedroom, the hotel bar, Charlottesville, Texas, Afghanistan, and Puerto Rico, the ego and the heart.

Read this book from beginning to end, and you will discover nothing short of a history of our times, "an old event unspooling itself," to use Reyna's own prescient words. Trump's brainless saber-rattling, with its echoes of Hitler and Mussolini and Jefferson Davis, appear on stage alongside flashes of life and love and humor, all comingling on the eve of what feels like end times. And yet, beneath the rage, beneath the cutting satirical tweets, beneath the relentless interrogation of the Trump women, this is a work of empathy in the best sense. Without apology, Reyna steps into the worlds of others and tries to feel her way into their pain, anger, and frustration, elusive as it might be. She animates Trump's base and reveals how their anguish and confusion were so easily mobilized by forces that didn't truly care about their well-being.

Reading Tea Leaves After Trump is also a work of mourning. Mourning is what we do when we grieve, and it is not always about loss or endings. I'm reminded of ACT-UP leader Douglas Crimp, who pointed out nearly thirty years ago that the activists fighting the AIDS pandemic were in a constant state of mourning, since they were losing friends, comrades, and lovers practically every day. But rather than lead to passivity and acceptance, the act of mourning inspired militancy and deepened their commitment to struggle.[1]

Like Crimp, Reyna understands what many of us do not: that we *must* mourn *and* organize. This is why the fifth and final act of this book, "Acceptance," resists closure. If the tea leaves tell us anything, it is that we have to make more tea. Trumpism is not the end of history. As Reyna states in one of her opening poems, "Novas blazed eternally yet disappear in blinks."

---

[1] Douglas Crimp, "Mourning and Militancy," *October* 51 (1989), 18.

Table of Contents

Stage 2: Anger

Stage 3: Negotiating

Stage 4: Depression

Stage 5: Acceptance

HOW TO READ TEA LEAVES

Start with white
for purity, clarity.
A white or ivory cup, sloping sides
for latitude in vision.
Fill cup with leaves loose, pure-picked,
for fullness when they soak and spread.

Add scalding water,
since decisions often come with fire and flame.
Grasp cup, your fingers pressing into china
as your questions seep through flesh,
through heat, into the swirl.
Drink gently, or deeply,
for water holds no answers.

Gaze at the darkness in the bottom:
limp leaves black and curled, clumped,
or sticking as isolated dots along the sides.
Close your eyes and fill your lungs.
Gaze inside you where your queries flail,
as the tea leaves did.
Know that all is hidden, all is
mere interpretation.

Reach back into the centuries
when kings and queens and peasants
were alike in not knowing,
when they had gazed at melted wax,

or melted lead, in not knowing.
Peer closely at the tea leaves in your cup:
animals, moons, stars, flowers,
or whatever you can make of them,
for what you think is what you see.

Denial

DENIAL*

In grief, Elisabeth says, we won't stow "messy emotions" into boxes.
Won't closet numbness like tinker toy niches that camouflage chaos.
We can't wrap grief up and hide it in dusty corners till examination
time.
No, she says. Grief tricks us, gauzes our eyes and ears
with disbelief.

And so it is.
No, she didn't lose, didn't lose the race, couldn't have. A deeper stab:
No, he didn't. Couldn't have won.
Couldn't
have
deluded
America.

We walk from here to there, stone pressed on chest, eyes dry.
How could this have happened? Over coffee, in smoky corners of dusky
bars, on porches scuffed with chairs pulled close, in water cooler
inquests, at dinner tables quiet with napkins unturned, in living rooms
dimmed with the TV off, in backyard bowers with stunned hammocks
swaying.

How can this be?
Elisabeth told us once before, told us this is how grief goes. How it
unfolds, step by step, hard moments backed up like monuments
mossed. This is how
grief steels itself
and stumbles on.

---

*Based on Elisabeth Kubler-Ross, MD, & David Kessler's "The Five Stages of
Grief." In *On Grief and Grieving: Finding the Meaning of Grief Through the Five
Stages of Loss.* (Simon & Shuster, 2005).

THIS

This is how words tremble through verse,
sprinkled with ink from a sundered heart.

This is how ash unfurls its skirts,
smoothing and stroking bones vapored in sun.

This is how loss is tucked into earth,
stuttering, stricken, like pearls unstrung.

NEW

New always attracts: new boyfriend, lover,
hairdo, home, new with or without new-car smells, new leases on
life, and all the rigamarole that clichés tell us represent *new*.

But old is new again, the old saw says, and news aren't
new when TV spews what the web spat out last night. New
is old when the car drives off the lot.

Habits hogtie us to old. New tattooes twist on shriveled skin
with pixillated saints ancient as myth. Demagogue darlings on stage
strut new Bruno Magli shoes and spout dogma calcified with lies.

Old is new and new is old. Novas blazed eternally yet disappear
in blinks. Wizards cast new spells, and medicine men plumb
ancestors' tales to cure the newborn babe.

New is old and old is new. The stripper dreams of adolescent loves and
haunts new bars across the way. Swollen rivers melt their Neolithic
banks in floods stoked by modernity.

Old new, new old, interwoven, stitched together in waves and
swirls, seemingly seamless, deluding and denuding, tricking us to
think we can pinpoint endings and beginnings.

CROOKED

He hung that word like a millstone 'round her neck and dragged her to her death. The letter A could not have soiled, could not have killed this woman faster or more surely.

But if she's crooked, curl me like plastic straws, twist me in the meanest knot, and write my name in her book of warriors.

If she's crooked, let me swab sweat from her brow and anoint it on my face that I might fight like her.

If she's crooked, let me bind her heart as it bled when two towers crumpled and heroes fled into flames.

If she's crooked, let me sit at her knee to watch her learn, head down with midnight books, immersed in details that spin men's heads.

If she's crooked, fill me with a fraction of her passion that I, too, might fly a million miles to comfort orphans in refugee tents and tell girls in dusty towns that they'll inherit this earth.

If she's crooked, grant me a cup of her courage, spine ramrod straight, as she parried little men's slanders in hearings from hell.

If she's crooked, fill me with one ounce of her tenacity through thirty years of tirades from men who trembled at her strength.

Crooked. Just a word, an instant word, concocted by a crooked man with a crooked past cooking crooked plans to convolute a billion lives contorted with lies.

But if she's crooked, fill me with a memory deep and long of her childhood path and how it diverged from his.

Let me count the hurts she healed, the lives she touched, the ceilings she cracked.

If she's crooked, heavens have lost their bearings, and no human being can be credible again.

INAUGURAL

(Sent with deep regrets by
Aki Kiwashimoto, aspiring haiku master,
to first-generation Trump)

inky skies   clouds black
   new president scowls words at
soaked heads   sudden rains

gray umbrellas wilt
  sun revolts against sparse lawn
   no one warm or safe

yellow hair flutters
    visions dark   streets swept in blood
boots in sand   bombs close

staccato words stab
   pout spits vows of coal and bans
     thunder punctuates

  cold slaps monuments
  stone fathers silent in shade
  marble pillars small

45th squints hard
uniforms tramp past his stand--
      his, *all*   only *his*

trump wanted missiles,
   tanks   like Russia's parades
     like North Korea

12 TWEETS

I talk you listen. Muhammad Ali wrong! I'm the GREATEST. Best US candidate in history! First to Make America Great! Huge beautiful changes.

Access Hollywood tape fake news! Liberal media unfair! Locker room talk, just joking with Billy! No assaults, women love me everywhere I go.

Huge victory in court! Trump U innocent, no fraud. Paid them to shut their lies up. No respect only lies. Trump U the greatest believe me.

Best transition team ever! Great mtgs. with Japan & India leaders. Ivanka & Jared made huge deals. No conflict, trust me! Great negotiators.

Trump Hotel in D.C. is the best! So many world leaders, great inauguration. Biggest inauguration in history, over 2 million people! Amazing!

Ivanka, Jared, Eric, Donald Jr. the greatest advisors believe me. Amazing blind trust. Big all over the world. Great meetings, huge deals.

No conflict of interest. I'm President! Can do anything I want, trust me. Will run my business & nation too. Hire the best & drain the swamp!

Melania greatest first lady in history, bigly! She'll live in NY, greatest place. First class all the way! Everyone wants to be like her.

Hamilton thugs should all be locked up with Crooked Hillary. No respect just lies. Paid agitators! Lock them up with CNN & the lying media.

Media all crooked liars, CNN the worst, no respect, paid agitators! Shut CNN down, shut Clinton Foundation, shut Hamilton. All crooks!

Melania's anti-bullying plan as first lady is the greatest. Better than any other first lady in history! Huge idea to fight bullying!

Media's huge lies about white nationalists! No salutes, KKK, or Nazi chants. Only paid agitators by media! Don't forget freedom of speech.

WHAT HITLER DID

He railed against economy rigs
Jews raking our money
Foreigners holding white men down
Nations dictating our affairs
Jobs gone
Factories shut
Coal taken away

White men reduced to less than

Face flushed, he spewed fear
Stoked hate of *the other*
Mocked war that left enemies alive
Surrounded himself with guns
Praised militia armed to their dragon teeth
Shouted what mobs wanted to hear
Promised to end white men's grief

White men elevated to the top

He scowled, frowned, shouted
Clown, charlatan, con man reviled
Joke of the establishment
Promised right-wingers would reign
Demanded absolute loyalty
Blindsided politicians
Tricked power into releasing power

Hooked blinders on his people's eyes
Kept blankets on his plots and thefts
Made his puppets complicit
Made them turn stone eyes to travesty

This man who would be emperor
Strides past columns in marble halls
Hears chants of 'Heil!' down the street
Arms raised in D.C. rally
Compatriot KKK in rooms nearby
This January day—
Trump smiles at them, thumbs-up

BASE

*"The media has come up short in telling the story of one side of that divide —
of the people experiencing anger, voicelessness and powerlessness."*
--Lydia Polgreen*

They mock my Bible, diner waitress says, blunt pencil tapping
        on her pad.
Three men sipping nod their heads and grunt.
They have no god, a farmer sighs, *men humping men, women being
        men, men growing breasts.*
What happens to their manhood? the plumber says to snorts and
        chuckles all around.
But underneath the banter and the nervous ease lies hurt.

Appalachia's glory, if it ever was, suffused to dust generations past.
The postman of the single shack, fingernails permanently black,
        shuffles to a chair and slouches in.
When I mined, I had money, he says flatly, *and a better house than now.*
He coughs in recollection.
Buddies died. Mines shut. Kids moved away. Now look what stayed.

If this mountain outpost were a mold, it would be cast a
        hundredfold in flatlands, hills, and desert towns criss-crossing
        coast to coast.
Sad songs are sung the same in far-flung haunts of ghosts and faded
        ways.
This is Trump's base: their angst, their pining for the past, their
        mourning for evaporated jobs, their unpinned moorings in
        the face of *change*—
their status lost. Or so they seem to think. Their status lost.
People perched atop hierarchies fall hardest.

35

White privilege lost, some say on the other side of the divide.
Can't handle losing that. Can't handle being minority, some say on the
        other side.
*White supremacy. Nationalism and Nazis. This is what Trump's base is
        drowning in,* say others in this great divide.
And the breach widens.
A shark mouth with razor teeth gnashes and gapes.

In quiet suburbs of the West, grandmothers cluster on a porch,
        bemoaning nanny states and internet indecency.
Factories closed before our husbands retired, one woman says.
Jobs off-shored.
*Our men gave their lifeblood to put roofs over our heads…before women's
        lib,* another sighs.
Trump's base: not Nazi but inhabiting an era shut and gone.

Trump's base: most didn't trust him, polls said.
Most didn't believe his lies, shrugged off his sex assaults and
        Trump U scams.
They packed rallies, donned his cliché cap, wore shirts extolling the
        man hoarding his tax returns.
Cheered his wild lies about lock-ups, border walls, bans, and
        bringing back the jobs (others) sent abroad.
They didn't care that he went bankrupt, threw F-bombs, urged
        violence, trashed women, Blacks, Mexicans, Muslims, and
        any un-Whites.
They embraced his spit and grit, tough-ass talk and push.
Mouth full of nails, words in-your-face, no apology, no grace.

Trump's base: no monolith, not educated to the max, not employed
　　　but most not poor, lacking in melanin and wedded
　　　to centuries past.
Embracers of destructors, haters of swamps, anti-elitist, anti-science,
　　　anti-facts.
A panoply of contradictions: worshipping the past, abhorring
　　　traditions; believers in laws but not ethics.
Hating corporate greed but voting for the billionaire who offshores
　　　it all, their billionaire who usurps charity funds and reneges on
　　　workers' contracts.
Trump's base: incontrovertibly inscrutable
in their side of the divide.

---

*"Letter from the Editor: HuffPost's New Chapter," 4. 25.17.

FLY:
AT THE BEGINNING OF CAMPAIGN

how bloated you must be   proxy eyes invisible ears
omnipotent   staying mum up in your corner of the wall
filled with what the rest of us don't know

what did the immigrant say back in her onyx
halls   sliding off the spandex dress and rail-spike heels
while he pot-bellied his way to bed still scowling at rapists

did she say i'm an immigrant too   you knew
me when i struggled   how can i pretend
not to have heard you say those things

or did she just slink into her satin gown
and yawn   and pretend never to have
been 'illegal' in America

did she take pills before slipping into bed
was she morose during sex as she is onscreen
did she shut her eyes as he kissed her with his pout

in mornings do they cuddle or does he wake up
scowling   does he ravage her before she has a
chance to go check on their son

FLY:
AT THE MIDDLE OF CAMPAIGN

did she bash him for grabbing strange-woman
crotch   for plunging his tongue into the
journalist's mouth   in his own daughter's room

while she upstairs   pregnant   changed from
one clinging dress into another for the
interview and photo shoot

did the immigrant throw her shoes at
him   slap him   spit at him when he
tried to pull her close to his belly

or did she pretend nothing happened
on TV today   no new scandals   nothing else
her husband did to her today

does she say it hurts   does she cry
or does she stay with mouth clamped tight
like on TV

does she have her own room

is this why the pretender stays awake
so late   three or four   plucking at keys
in twitter fits   and does she approve

FLY:
AT THE END OF CAMPAIGN

does he ever read a book   do the two of them
eat breakfast with their son
and does she ever say she wants to hide

does she wish her dresses weren't so tight
when she grooms once he's gone   or her
heels so high   does she say they hurt

does she turn her face when he lies onscreen
or say to him he lies too much   or does she
tell him not to say cruel things to others

or is she always silent   does he say to her
stay out of my affairs   *my* campaign
you're here because of *me* and only *me*

did she weep when he won   did she excuse
herself from the celebration and lie down
alone in her darkened room   sobbing

or did she laugh and drink and say how proud
she was of him   then slink from bed and cry
when he finally fell asleep that night

HEADLINE NEWS:
TRUMP'S CHOICES TO RUN THE NATION*

**Trump Nominates Housing Predator,
"Foreclosure King," as Secretary of Treasury**

**Trump Taps Billionaire Known as "Bankruptcy King,"
Who Owned Deadly Coal Mine, as Commerce Secretary**

**Trump's Choice for Attorney General:
Opposed Law Protecting Disabled Children,
Supports Voter Suppression, Opposes Civil Rights**

Trump's selection for **Department of Health & Human Services** plans to slash or dismantle Medicare, Medicaid, Social Security, children's health insurance, Obamacare, women's healthcare rights, and anti-discrimination laws. Bought medical stock then presented legislation in U.S. Congress to benefit the company and his own pockets.

**Trump's 3 Candidates, Secretary of State:
Convicted Adulterer & Giver of Classified Info to Mistress,
Serial Adulterer with Zero Foreign Policy Experience,
Failed Politician Who Believes in "Magic Underwear" & "Magic Planets"**

**A Trump Candidate for Homeland Security Boss:
Sheriff of Deadly Jail Where Women & Children
Detainees Died Under His Watch**

**Trump's Choice for Secretary of Interior: Climate Change Denier,
Hater of Clean Energy, Lover of Dirty Coal,
Enabler of Water & Air Polluters, Opponent of Public Protected Lands**

Trump's Choice for Secretary of Education:
Billionaire Donor Intent on Dismantling Public Schools,
Use Taxpayer Money to Fund Kids' Private Education

Trump's Choice for Secretary of Housing:
Man Whose Knowledge of Housing Issues
Is "I Used to Live in Detroit Once"

Trump's promise to **"drain the swamp"** now questionable as he names 6 billionaires to top jobs, raids Goldman Sachs & Wall Street for Cabinet picks and advisor slots. None with experience in military, government, or in jobs for which chosen.

Trump's Nominee for Department of Energy
Wanted to Kill Agency, Denies Climate Science,
Believes Earth is 6,000 Years Old

Secretary of Labor Nominee Bashes Unions,
Abuses Workers, Opposes Minimum Wage

Trump Nominates Mitch McConnell's Wife
as Secretary of Transportation

---

*All information above based on actual headlines and news stories, Fall 2016. By the end of the first month of Trump's presidency, almost all these candidates had been confirmed.

KELLYANNE

1

She speaks in honeyed tones, syrup words dripping in measured
droplets meant to mollify her boss' rage and keep the herd reined in.

Pointy chin up, smile stenciled tight, she looks staunchly at the lens
and does the pollster thing: sound bites spun this way and that,
whatever fits, omissions and commissions, whatever snares and turns
heads where she wants.

On screen she pivots and deflects. Journalists can't break the wax
façade, her parries, sidesteps, and touchés that lurch their commentary
off the script. *Facts are not facts,* she drips, and unwinds stories from her
mind, allegations based on myth: Bowling Green Massacre, terrorists
unreported, the hugeness of her boss' crowds.

Perhaps she thinks a silky voice erases lies. Perhaps she thinks a face
unflustered, calmness painted with bedraggled strokes, can trick. Her
words delude, denuding truth in every phrase, every doublespeak that
slithers from her lips. *He won because he was superior,* she intones, her
stony smile convinced she'll be believed.

2

Not long ago she hated this pretender, Cruz' rival, loathed his sham
claims, his offensive ramrodding of the little guy.

It's been a rough road here, to this child-man space, where eternal
mothering is her cross. Farmlands to Jersey shores, she's been toughed
up, and birthed 4 girls, and for years polled through politicians till she
hit the top. *You can have any job you want,* boss said as she carted boxes
to the western wing. *Any job you want.*

So here she is, coddling the man who shocked the world, cooing to him in dulcet praise, soothing his infinite ruffled feathers and lambasting the pesky protestors who throw boss into orange rage.

She learned from toddlers how to squelch White House tantrums, how to twist truth slyly to lull the angry one into submission.

Biographical information: Wikipedia, "Kellyanne Conway."
Conway became Trump's presidential campaign manager when Paul Manafort resigned, then became a senior advisor in the White House after the election. She once said publicly that she used child management strategies similar to what she used with her four young daughters to appease and calm Trump.

HER DAUGHTERS

4 girls she has at home: 4 girls who watch and listen
    girls who'll grow up in a loud man's land
4 girls who see her gallop to keep the madman calm
    girls who see her pander, just to stay on top
4 girls who know their mother is superior to her boss
    girls who cringe when he comes near them, or her
4 girls who ponder daily how she concocts her lies
    girls who sit in Sunday school and pray to Christ

Memo

TO: Mrs. Kellyanne Conway
FROM: Miss Mildred Alice Masterson *MAM*
RE: Role Modeling

Mrs. Conway, please pardon my use of a memo in lieu of a formal letter. My scruples as a doting grandmother and lifelong schoolteacher did not allow me to address you as 'dear' in fear that, if you somehow discerned my opinion of you, my greeting to you as such would soon reveal itself to have been ersatz respect.

My predilection is on the conservative, traditional side of manners, which is partly why I'm a lifelong Republican, with an unshakeable affinity for 'conservative.' This is the first time that I have composed any type of missive to a governmental entity, but I am hopeful that I'll be able to relay my sentiments in clear, cogent phrasing.

To thrust to the crux: Do you regularly contemplate the role of parental modeling in children's intellectual, mental, emotional, and spiritual evolution? I pose this query because I know you were a stellar student, receiving your law degree *magna cum laude;* thus there is no shortage of intellect in you, so you are undoubtedly aware of psychological theories regarding role modeling. Therefore the key word in my question is 'regularly.'

To speak bluntly: I am concerned about your four lovely daughters. They are fragile souls whose core identities are developing quite rapidly. I am consumed by worry that your girls are learning that women who rise in power must metamorphose to reflect the indiscretions and foibles of the men whom they serve. Since women are notably scarce in the White House 'team' (I dislike the manly sound of that!), I can somewhat understand that you've had to push your feminine gentleness aside to be tough, or appear sufficiently feisty, to fit your boss' expectations. Ignoring maternal instincts must be devastating to you, Mrs. Conway! My sympathies.

But I pray: Please be cognizant of what your girls are learning each time they see you on television, each time they hear you being interviewed, or each time they read your commentary in newspapers. Unfortunately, men can be unconscionable in speech or innuendos, but we women cannot be their parrots. They trudge on unscathed (as per your boss), but women are not forgiven.

Don't sink, Mrs. Conway. Role modeling is not a pittance we recall every now and then. Please rise above. Not for him but for your girls.

Thank you for your kind attention to my words, and for your service to our great nation.

#   #   #

MARTIN, FROM THE GRAVE

If I could turn, I would, but this coffin holds me still. I whisper to you now through fifty years of tears for what you have endured.

We've marched these sizzling streets before, these bridges blocked by dogs, batons, and helmets of hate.

We've pitched these battles before, teeth tearing ankles, rubber bullets burning backs, clubs dense as rifle butts cracking skulls.

We've locked arms, locked eyes, locked hands on heads for safety when they came with boots and hoses to shut us down. We've dragged cheeks and chins on concrete when they pulled us by our feet across blood-stained streets.

We've been shot unarmed, flayed to the bone, hanged like dead rabbits by back doors, white folks picnicking by trees where our mangled bodies turned in air, photo ops galore. We've seen the photos in their stores.

If I could spin, I would, for what they did, what they do, should've died decades past but won't. So my rasp will filter like earthworms through these clods, through stones, through dirt less dirty than the bludgeoners, through smoke of churches burnt, through ether and miasmas of stillborn hopes, through centuries of hacking on the shackles. No amount of blood we shed can satiate their hate.

I whisper to you now through fifty years of hush, for I hear boots tramping once again, their boots, and smell the Ku Klux stench in the People's House. I rush my rasp to you right now, for I hear the

rattle of chains in Koch Brother laws, hear our ballots torn and
tossed, hear us mocked again for marching arm-in-arm.

I send my rasp to you, from here, for I see ramrod arms stretched
high, and the man who would be king tell daily lies, and see
billionaires with secrets taking reins. I whisper to you now, from
here, for I see zealots in towers and lounging by lakes, our people's
money raked into pockets mysterious and soiled.

You've stared in these men's eyes before, withstood forked tongues
that turn equality to roulette wheels. You've heard their codes and
veiled slurs, taken shields against these wars. If you can hear my
whisper, remember what my heart once said: The measure of a
man is where he stands at times of challenge and despair. Today
these heartbreaks bore to the core of earth.

If I could spin or turn, I would. My coffin keeps me prisoned while
my spirit weeps for you. My dessicated eyes, vacant mouth, tired
ears filled with dust ceased mattering on that balcony in spring.
My lips are stilled and my dust is mixed with worms, but your feet
hold fire, your arms still link, and your voices are oceans
unleashed.

IMMIGRATION

Nothing runs deeper than human roots.

But funny how courage to rend bonds,
to cleave from elders and brothers,
from healers, tribesmen,
imams that soothed us or Omas that cradled,
has no nation,
no year,
no boundary to keep us root-bound.

Funny how we spar with oceans or desert devils,
jungles and endless sun,
storms, snowdrifts or white waters,
and how these cannot wrestle us down,
headlock us, pin us to ground,
beaten away from dreams.

Funny how briars or fences,
walls made of stone, razor steel, mountains,
ditches dug putrid and deep,
guns guarding exits
or volts killing hearts
cannot squelch quests for new lives.

Funny how desire to flourish
swells in our breasts,
blooms, expands,
nurturing visions bounteous and safe,
how color or history are quickly erased.

Nothing runs stronger than human will.

But funny how signers of papers
and pounders of gavels
raise hands in their chambers
and spout lengthy speeches,
deluding their voters and touting false vows
to curb and extinguish migration.

Funny how these signers and pounders
are flesh, bone and sinew,
muscle and blood,
of ancestral mothers pale and huddled
in boats tossed on oceans,
birthing their sons
in colonies circled
by tree trunks denuded and sharp,
birthing their babies in forts fending off
aboriginal horsemen
in feathers and buffalo skins.

Funny how these travelers
came of their will across big seas,
in journeys long and dark,
without compact,
without invitation or welcoming arms,
without papers or testaments,
without court decrees of indisputable rights
to seductive alien lands
swarming, stealing, settling, claiming.

Funny how rulers reinvent roots*,
pretend they sprang newborn
from mystical genes

on American soil,
negating their alien beginnings,
blotting ancestor migrants
whose tongues unfurled foreign words,
who struggled in shadows,
poor and displaced,
decades and centuries past.

---

* Trump's mother was an immigrant to the United States from Scotland. His paternal grandparents were immigrants to America from Germany. Trump's first wife, Ivana, was an immigrant to the U.S. from Czechoslovakia; therefore, Trump's daughter Ivanka, and sons Don Jr. and Eric, are all children of an immigrant. Trump's third wife, Melania, was an immigrant to the U.S. from Slovenia and reportedly did not become a naturalized citizen until after her son's birth. Her son, Barron, is, as his siblings, a son of an immigrant. [Information collated and adapted from Wikipedia, "Donald Trump."]

Thus, Trump and all of his immediate family—wife, sons, daughter, and grandchildren—are descendants of immigrants, either first-generation or second- and third-generation. This fact bewilders many people who consider Trump's family history to be immigrant-centric and thus are confounded by Trump's commentaries against immigrants.

Dear Mr. President Trump –

I'm a farmer in Kentucky, lifelong GOP, me and my family as far back as we recall. Served in 'Nam, infantry, got as high as Master Sgt. when I left the army and went back to the family farm. I have a sharpshooter medal, one of the best in my unit, and two purple hearts, but I'd give them up right now if you read this letter and please listen to a combat vet!

I still have nightmares from 'Nam, Mr. President. I know you had some foot problems serious enough for you to get excused from the war. I hope you're healed now. Folks in town say you suffered a lot and you really wanted to go serve your country, but your disabilities kept you away and that's why you love the military so much. Thanks, sir, for loving us soldiers. War is hell, pardon my language. But the deaths I saw in 8 years of combat don't compare to what we have in our homeland here.

When all those kids back east died at their school, shot to death, I cried all day. Then the Muslims in California shooting their fellow workers, and yeah, I prayed a lot when that lady Gabby got shot in the head in Arizona, then the theatre shooting after that, and on and on. The Columbine school killings so long ago now seem like small potatoes, sad to say.

Speaking as an army man really good with guns, all

those killers here in the USA massacring with assault rifles boils my blood. <u>WE</u> had those guns and killed dozens of commies in minutes. Assault rifles were never created for civilians and they don't belong in people's hands.

Please, Pres. Trump. I know liberals say you hate listening to people, but I can't believe that. Time to put millions of American lives, like mine, higher on your priority list than NRA. I cancelled on them after the little school kids tragedy. NRA used to care about good regulations, now they want zero restrictions and 100% percent power.

Please push them aside, sir, tell them to go jump in the lake. Force Congress to pass gun control on assault rifles. If you do nothing but that regarding guns, it's enough. 2nd Amendment existed just fine way before auto weapons were put in the people's hands, and the 2nd will be just fine when the AR's are given back only to soldiers and cops.

Please, sir, I'm begging you.

Respectfully yours,
John Keith Haggerty

SHADOW LOVE

I don't recall when we first spoke, but I
remember how his tall frame
ambled by my café table
that first time, and he stalled beside my chair,
his reflection in the glass across the room
so filled with grace, with quiet wonderment.
I looked straight ahead, unmoving,
breath held.

The book he carried snagged my heart:
Reading Lolita in Tehran —
clash of cultures: one group loving from afar,
from the shadows, loving the forbidden,
fearing disaster and braving the chance of
everything falling apart.

He didn't speak and for days
pretended not to notice me, there,
just feet away beside the window
where he could see my face
no matter where he sat.

I smelled the thick black coffee
he preferred, heavy pastries held lightly
in fingers slender and slow,
watched him licking icing from scones,
frowning in his coffee cup,
deciphering how he
could hear my breath, miles away.

One day our fingers brushed
as we reached, blushing,
for napkins at counter's end.
Reading Lolita, pages bent, dog-eared,
lay on the table by my hand.
My blood pulsated in my head.
He spoke and broke the barricade we'd had.
His heavy accent, bumbling words, deep red face—
but his gaze spoke words that tripped his tongue.
Love at first sight,
love from out the shadows,
shadow love.

He was alien, undocumented, illegal.
Poems he whispered as we lay
in dusky rooms spoke of love, forgiveness,
the preciousness of time,
children's breath,
the dark loneliness of death.
But like the reading of *Lolita,*
we loved on borrowed time,
in stealth and furtive hours,
aware of risks
and how things fall apart.
Love without papers
is hard.

Anger

ANGER*

The red roiling in my gut defies tears and words.
Don't try to soothe, to rub your salves on my face and head,
      to sprinkle your satin pablum on these flames.
Take your arm off my shoulder, slide your aromatic teacups
      back to your side of the table.
Crumple in a corner if you wish, for my legs won't uncurl from this
      fetal stage tonight,
and maybe not tomorrow or tomorrow or next week.

Remember faces on the TV screen, mouths wailing, heads lost in
      sleeves and laps,
bodies melted to carpets and quaking, questioning arms.
Remember hushed streets, eyes wide, hands hiding shaking lips.
Watching from warmth of sofas or happy bars or celebration
      ballrooms,
we didn't survive the horror of hurtling trains,
state-by-state runaway rogues that came from dankest corners of
      what we thought was home,
what we thought was history, equality, sanity.

Our nation lost, our nation's lost, our nation's not my nation
      anymore.
Some things don't need a coffin when they're dead and gone.
Some things die to dissipate their vapor-poison months on end.
I won't wear black, won't pray, for God is dead.
Betrayed like an abandoned bride, I'll rage in quiet rooms, beat
      pillows to a pulp,
and know that weakness beat us—beat us *all*—to dust.

---

*According to Elisabeth Kubler-Ross, anger is the second stage of loss.

ALTERNATIVES

Facts are alternative don't you know. Liberty is freedom and choice comes with freedom (no not *that* choice!) and "choices" are "alternatives" and choices must be freely grabbed and alternatives give us freedom and freedom is liberty.

Facts are important but not as bigly as freedom so facts have to be free to be important and you can't be free if you have no choices or alternatives so facts can't be cement because cement gives no freedom of movement and you get locked in and there goes your freedom.

So important facts are alternative because it was the freedom to shape them that gave them shape and meaning and this meaning has to be freely given for there to be freedom so there you have it.

Yes we care about facts and that's why their meaning has to mean something important to us and why alternative facts are best.

HIS TWEETS | THEIR MARCH

My inauguration crowd much bigger than marcher thugs, biggest, best audience in history! Standing ovations! Bad losers need to get over it!

Greatest inauguration speech ever, better than Obama. Bigger crowd than Obama. Loser marchers, wasting time. Should've gone out to vote!

Where were they on election day? Losers, unpatriotic, disrespectful. Violent thugs marching, who cares? Don't forget who won by landslide!

Paid agitators behind it all. Loser Hillary paid them. Un-American thugs should all be locked up! Disgrace to our country & the whole world!

CNN & lying media not right! My inaug. crowds much bigger, biggest in history. Over 2 million!! Adoring crowds. They love me, I love them!

No nation can tell me what to do! Who cares what foreigners think? I won by a landslide, biggest victory ever in U.S. history! Stop whining!

Marchers are thugs, should be charged with crime. Arrest them & lock them up! Lock Hillary up, biggest loser, paying people $1000 to march!

I'm U.S. President, not foreigners. Who cares what thugs in rest of the world think? Rigged marches, clueless foreigners! They are nothing!!

TWEETS, THE "WOMEN'S MARCH": JANUARY 21, 2017*

For 1st time since election, I wept. Hugged everyone, linked arms, had great time, full solidarity. So good to see I'm not mourning alone!

Women's march = show of force for who U.S. is! Loved reading all the handmade posters, so many issues, deep caring! Felt good to be out there!

Women's march? Yes but joined by men, children, ppl of all colors. Beautiful sight! THIS is the "real America" for the whole world to see!

Met 90-yr old marcher, Anna, walking w/ cane. Big pussy hat she knit herself! She's marching for her daughter, who passed away last year.

Pressed tight, shoulder to shoulder, all peaceful! Energy is amazing! Cried most of the day. We r raising our voices in peace & democracy.

Women in wheelchairs, men with canes, little girls with posters. Babies on dads' shoulders. Nothing can stop us. Best experience of my life!

Boston, 100,000+ and growing! Lots of men. My wife made me a pussy hat. Proud wearing it, like many other men. Women's rights = human rights!

Marched 4 Hillary & history she almost made. But we r making history today, my daughter, millions of ppl around world! Am crying with joy!

My soul is healed. Our spirits are soothed. Together we washed away our grief. We will defy. We will prevail. America won't be lost.

---

* The "Women's March" the day after Trump's inauguration became the largest protest in United States history, and one of the largest in the world, with 673 cities bringing almost 5 million marchers into streets nationally and globally. In Washington, D.C. alone—the heart and origin point of the protests—590,000 protestors filled the city, many marching shoulder-to-shoulder through most of the day, the first official day of the Trump administration. Protestors from over 82 nations in *all 7 continents of earth, including Antarctica,* also participated. The numbers were huge in large cities around the world: e.g., 625,000 in Los Angeles. Men, children, transgender individuals, and protestors of all generations and cultures marched, carrying protest signs addressing every major sociopolitical issue today.

This historic march was largely organized by four diverse American women activists: a Muslim Palestinian-American, an African-American, a Latina, and a White activist. (Information from *Rise Up! The Women's Marches Around the World:* Condé Nast Special Commemorative Edition, 11.5.17.)

MARTIN, AGAIN

My fellow Americans, I am about to burst forth from my coffin. I had a dream last night, a dream that shook the very foundations of my still-alive soul, for a good man's soul is not extinguished like a candle flame pinched shut. Its light radiates beyond the grave. At least I like to think this is the case.

I had a dream that a descendant of KKK lynchers is in line for a high post in the House: lawman supreme, lawman for the people of America, seeker of equality for all, interpreter of laws and leveler of playing fields for all colors, all tongues. Equal. Equal in the eyes of Lady Justice, she, blind to bias, with the scales held high.

Descendant by blood, I don't know. But descendant by character, yes, sadly yes, sadly this man is. He has pushed his boots on black voters' backs, I dreamt. He deems sexual diversity proof of deviance devised by devils. He banishes to hell any woman who clasps authority to the god-given domain of her body. There is scarce justice in his bones.

My fellow Americans, I had a dream last night, and it shook my faith in man. I dreamt a billionaire swimming in a garnet pool of foreign cash, the bills glowing so red, they seemed as blood, fresh blood. Yet this white-haired man smiled large, swam with ease, as if red cash were his water, his element of existence.

He floated from the pool, designer suit stone-dry and punctuated on lapels with pins: one each side, one with stripes and stars, the other ruby red with a stick-handled moon. Paper bills stuck to pockets, sleeves, front, back, waved in slight breezes as he walked onto a broad gray map glued on the concrete deck: a map of the world.

My fellow Americans, I had a dream last night, a dream that sat like a millstone on my breast, crushing breath and bones, a millstone that replicated itself millions of times, spinning and rasping in its gyrations, lumbering away from my coffin, into sky and clouds, like alien ships, landing among the populace around their necks.

Be still, my heart, be brave. And yours as well, America. For in my dreams I see vapors wafting like thieves across fields and towns and church steeples, above ponds and lakes, around pines that stab clouds, and the vapors mix among the people, settling like wet sheets across their faces, arms, legs, chests, blinding, suffocating.

Be brave, America. Remember your legs, and march march march day in, day out. Remember your voices and lift them with passion wherever humanity gathers to renew vows to democracy. Remember your hands and write sturdy messages of love and hope to one another on protest signs as you march for our collective humanity.

LAST CALL

*Poll reveals shocking number of relationships that ended
because of the 2016 election.*
--AOL News, 2.7.17

The post-rain garden beckoned me outdoors. Glassene drops dot stems
and undersides of leaves. Dark earth embraces frail weeds and moss
through loam, sprinkling flower beds with green as far as eyes can
reach.

I greeted each tree, each bush, each plant, looked in their eyes, soul to
soul. Tulips dipped heads in recognition. Lantana swayed yellow skirts
and leaned on blue fescue between dances. Side-yard succulents
gleamed sunnily beside barrels of golden cacti.

My brother died today, an hour after his last call. Halting rasps of
tiredness. Staccato silence with shallow breaths. *So sorry*, he said, that
he'd cut me from his life. Hospital noises backdrop to his breathing.
Waiting to gather another sentence to say to me. *Never should have given
in to politics and hate*, he said.

Childhoods of desert hills and warm gulf waves. Confabs on porch
roofs after midnight under Texas stars, lumpy pillows propped on
haggard shingles on the slope. Laughing at Lucy and Ricky Ricardo
after school, cross-legged on the bare scuffed floor with a bowl of dry
Post Toasties at our feet.

We never should have given in to politics and hate. Raindrops tapped
and lashed as I listened to his breathing. His silence. Shared lives lived
in a dusty little town. Generations of birthing and dying, funerals and
birthdays, growing away by miles and decades. Still close, favorite
siblings, he and I, connected at the breast.

Until the windswept yellow hair came down the escalator in his tower. Like Moses' ocean cleaving into two, a wide swath of earth between, our politics lay down a demarcation not to cross. Two years of cleaving. Never should have given in to politics and hate.

Rains were merciless today, loud fingers thrumming as we said last words. Illness kept hidden, creeping out now, amidst rain, as he struggled.

The clouds' tears ceased an hour ago. Like lemmings, my legs took me to the garden. My salve. My zen. Leaves and blooms don't judge. Secrets guarded. Soul soothed. Inanities of humans erased in loam and mist, black earth, crystal droplets, and flowers that dip their heads.

Dear Sis,

I asked Marian to give you this letter after I'm gone. I never had the courage to tell you these things while I was still alive. But I think you should know. As mom always used to say, "Better late than never!" [I know you hate clichés but I'm hoping you'll forgive a sick man at this point.]

I don't know where to begin. I know when I pushed you out of my life, because I marked it in my journal. It was August 16, 2015, two months after my political hero (I won't mention his name!) announced he was running for president. I liked his dramatic flair, coming down his shiny escalator in his tower. That made an impression on me.

From the start, you and I butted heads, and it hurt me that you hated him so much. That's how I interpreted your criticisms of him. I liked his flashy style, his views, and his promises to us to make our nation great again. It made me sad that you couldn't see how great all the things he said were, and how much the American people idolized him and agreed with him. To me, you were the same-old, same-old super-liberal, though you say you're moderate. I swear you were a hardhead!

As you now know, my last year was sheer hell with this fluke disease. I apologize for not telling you about it. I sometimes felt you would've wanted to know, but I was angry at you for not understanding my views and wanted to punish you. We hadn't talked since August, when I cut you off, so I finally decided you wouldn't care anymore. We were too far gone.

68

Sis, I think now the real reason for all this was I wanted your approval. Your rejection of my opinions (and what I considered my values) felt to me like a rejection of my _self_. Like I wasn't smart enough to see what you saw. I wasn't smart enough to understand good and bad ideas. I felt inferior. You're my big sister, and I always looked up to you. I wanted your approval but couldn't say it. Why? I don't know. Machismo? Pride, feeling embarrassed? I felt dumb.

The point is, I wish I had listened when you said to me last August that politics are immaterial and we shouldn't reject each other because of our differences. But I was too angry at you and blew you off. I apologize.

We were the closest siblings in our whole family. Gee whiz! Five kids and we were the closest. Now here I am, and I'll die alone, with just my wife Marian and not you, and all for politics. I'm crying a little bit right now because I miss you and I know you'd hold my hand if you were here, and we could laugh about all the fun things we did, the silly fights we had, all the games we played, and the time you climbed that tall mesquite tree in the alley and couldn't get back down, and I threw ropes to you, and you finally got to the ground and you cried and vowed you weren't never, ever climbing trees again. And you never did!

Damn! I should have remembered that: you always knew how you felt and if you committed, you stuck to it. I should have known politics weren't different. I feel clueless. I wonder how many other people out there made this same mistake——banishing family for a stranger that doesn't even know us and might not even give a damn about you or me. So far, it seems that way.

But I'll be watching from the clouds, Sis. I bought my ticket, knew what I was getting into, and it was pricey! I put my faith in him and not you. I gambled. Goddamit, he better be the greatest president ever, and he better not screw up. If I can send thunderbolts down from the sky to strike him down if he messes up, I will. I promise you, I will.

Feel free to tear this letter up when you're done. I don't mean to make you feel bad, or feel sorry for me. I don't blame anyone. May God always bless you and your little family. I've missed out on so much. Please say a prayer for me, Sis, but above all....

Please forgive me.

My eternal love,
Miguel

WIFE-BEATER

"We're gonna have to have some dark days before we get to the blue sky
of morning again in America. We are going to have to take some massive pain."
--Steve Bannon, Interview, 2010*

1. 1996

Wife-beater knows all about pain--screaming welts on face and chest
when he throws his woman like a dog's doll against walls, onto floors,
through the window of a car. Her pain.

Knows how to bind his fingers on her throat like he pinzers bottles of
beer, knows how to vault over her body on the rug to rip the phone
from her and smash it on the door. Her pain.

Wife-beater knows how to coil and slither and fork his tongue at
cops with pencils poised, knows how to twist her words to obfuscate,
knows how to slap truth down.

Wife-beater knows dark days from years of crafting them, of filling her
with fear of him, shrinking her to a cur curled by the curb, someone
who flees his threats of darker days, and more massive pain.

2. 2017

Wife-beater puffs his bloated belly as he commandeers the throne,
eyes half-shut in TV lights, stubble face blotched red with alcohol
and hubris as the   Right. Hand. Man.

It's war, he growls. *It's war. Every day America's at war, America's
at war, we're at war.* He inhales, mouth closed, apocalyptic eyes
pinned on the war he plans for three years hence.

War is inevitable, he whispers in usurper's ears. *Pain is inevitable,*
he urges the pretender as he hands the pen to him. *And if the planet
dies, then so be it.*

Wife-beater watches as the don signs orders in the heat of camera
lights, papers dark and weighted down with vows, papers years in
crafting by the   Right   Hand   Man.

Wife-beater waddles to his room each night, drunk with sitting at the
hand of god, mammon god, the only god, and he dreams of blue sky
mornings tainted and tinted orange with flame.

---
* "Steve Bannon Believes the Apocalypse Is Coming and War Is Inevitable," by Paul
Blumenthal & JM Rieger. *Huffington Post,* 2.18.17. He predicted the U.S. would be
at war with China within three years. His 1996 spousal abuse was described in
various national news sources, including *The New Yorker* in 10.30.17.

TWO STEVES

Trump got a package deal:
two Steves connected at the hip,
no need to separate.
Bannon/Miller, Miller/Bannon.
Not quite the lyrical renown
of Rosencrantz & Gildenstern,
but same vibe.

Breitbart breast-fed,
Breitbart-bred,
two Steves whose brains were likewise boiled
in conspiracies and apocalyptic stews.

One writes Orders for his lord,
the other covers with clouds of lies.
One's florid face salivates at war,
the other decrees his lord above law.
Don't shoot the WH messengers,
but Bannoncrantz & Millerstern
are trapped in the wrong warp.

Trump got a package deal,
negotiator that he is,
going for cheap volume price,
double-deal, half-off,
making our country great with business skills,
America first, behind two conspirators whispering dark.

LOW-INFO VOTERS

One man one vote was our nation's curse
When that man lacked facts or common sense
When that man was blind and deaf and saw
Grabbing strange woman's crotch as strength

One man one vote was our nation's curse
When that man thought billions equated with brains
When he fell for the huckster's choreographed lies
And concluded that worth sprang from fame

One man one vote was our nation's curse
When that man was trapped in times long dead
In eras of King Coal and white man's rule
When the man let racism soak in his head

Multiply him by millions and millions more
Casting that ballot began the decline
Blindered and snookered and led by the nose
They voted for Con Don one man (one vote)   at   a   time

PRAYER: MELBOURNE, FL
2/18/17

Absent 3 weeks, she appears miraculously at his rally, the reluctant tourist in First Lady land, reclusive queen of the West—she who seeks to fade into curtained chambers, who loathes limelights, she who had chosen another life.

But here she is tsunamied with a thousand roars, her fingers quaking on the page he doesn't know she'd bring, he hovering behind her, skulking, scowling, eager to commandeer the podium, basking in the apoplexies of his base.

She trembles to the mike and reads the words as something just unearthed, halting, her tongue not hiding its Slovene.

The immigrant leads anti-immigrants in prayer:

> *Our Father who art in heaven,*
> *Hallowed be thy name.*

[We pray without constraints while Muslims fill with fear.]

> *Thy kingdom come.*
> *Thy will be done*
> *on earth as it is in heaven.*

[Who knows thy will? And does he care.]

> *Give us this day our daily bread,*

[The billionaire begrudges food stamps and raids labor camps.]

and forgive us our trespasses,
as we forgive those who trespass against us,
[Their breasts, crotch, their mouth with his tongue raping throats, and
hands like spiders spinning filth.]

and lead us not into temptation,
[They say golden showers, young girls, not one but more, and Putin
holds black cards in dossiers.]

but deliver us from evil.
[Can iron threads webbed deep in dirt be pulled?]

For thine is the kingdom,
and the power, and the glory, forever.
[First king, he says, elbows on the office desk, and laughs.]

Amen.
[Like a Greek chorus, his aides reply amen.]

ME FIRST

"I have only one rule: Me first, nobody second."
--Stated by a character, Nick Evers,
played by Roddy McDowell, in the movie, "Five-Card Stud," 1968.

Classic western flick had it all—brawls, accusations, gamblers, betrayal, mass murder, and a madam making sure the lust of narcissists got satiated. Gotta take care of those paying you.

Good 'ole Nick Evers, the saucy little guy with the big mouth and delusions. Had it all pegged out, me first, me and only me, all for me, none for you, me, me, all me.

With such a violent stew, gotta have Christ in there somewhere, too: Bible in the preacher's hand, hot derringer keeping company with proverbs and loving your neighbor above yourself.

Just celluloid, all this. Back when hippies shoved flowers in real rifles, and kids went to jungles and were blown apart by ghosts in palm fronds, napalm melting the skin off little girls.

Just celluloid. Tonight we watch these Hollywood honchos tracking down a self-anointed avenger, death's angel, the twisted man who sold his soul to shred others.

Tonight we watch Martin, McDowell, Mitchum, de Corsia, and sundry misfits make believe, swagger on screen, and deliver mock deaths, flickers of Netflix throbbing on dark walls.

Yesterday, Meadows, McCarthy, McSally, Curbelo, Ryan, and 212 gamblers swaggered on C-SPAN, inveighed for *liberty and freedom* on congressional carpet, and delivered death.

Had to take care of those paying, those stuffing millions in spandex pockets, had to satiate lobbers. Put god in with premeditated murder, mixed up real good with neighbors.

GOP avengers pandered their souls, stole survival from babies with holes in their hearts, slammed hospital doors on men with canes, and yanked life-saving tubes from cancerous throats.

Yesterday* good 'ole Nick Evers was there in D.C., his litany of me, me, me and only me more sticky and deadly in carpeted halls than celluloid killers and make-believe brawls.

---

*Yesterday: May 4, 2017, when the US House of Representatives passed a bill to repeal and replace Obamacare, stripping tens of millions of Americans of their health insurance. The repeal bill subsequently failed in the US Senate.

HUNGER

I can take the grumbles, the groans that gurgle in my stomach morning,
night, and throughout long hours at my desk.
I can take my belly sticking to itself inside.
I can take this.
As a child in little Texas towns, field to field, I learned that food is not a
given, work doesn't magically bring food, and some of us aren't meant
to eat as others do.
I can take this.

My father's back was black from sun, my mother's hands like broken
stone. My own were criss-crossed red from cotton bolls, sharp leaves,
and thorns.
Your hands weren't meant for pencils, mama said, *or for kissing,* papa
 muttered as he sat on dirt at noon. But he pressed my fingers to his
lips, and smiled, and took a bite of bread.
I could take it, eating like birds, working like horses, pushing tired
bones.
We piled on quilts spread on the floor at night and hummed
grandmother's songs to stave our hunger.
We all took it, stripped of hearts but beating on.

But my children are a different test.
They look out dusty glass on windows high above the street, Chicago
lights just twinkling on in shops and sidewalks far below, the long
night just unwinding.
My boy and girl have drunk their cup of milk, and eaten the
sandwich they split.
I gave them crackers in cellophane I picked up at the deli kiosk at my
job.

They lie like urchins in my bed, two stowaways with legs entwined like twigs, and cold bellies grumbling under the blanket that used to be mine.

When our room is black and still, neons blinking half a block away, with alley drunks passed out below, I wonder at the world.
I wonder at this world, at how it takes and takes and takes, at how our bones can break in toil, and our hearts collapse, and our spirits dessicate, without a murmur of protest.

I wonder at this world, at how children lie in cribs, or sit at desks, or lean on stoops with bellies vacant and souls the same, and how the world goes on.
I can take it, for myself.
I can take it.
But children…children…*oh, children.*

BETSY De VORCED

she says *De Vos*
wanders lost through school halls
thinking she's with congregants in choir robes
absently pulls out bibles to show teachers
education done right

she says *De Vos*
knows no laws protecting kids
in wheelchairs   boygirls scared of bathrooms
college teens fleeced nude by profit
doesn't know stomachs grumble loudest in class

she says *De Vos*
envisions textbooks bursting into flame
science turned to ash   history writ large and white
with prophet words extolling snakes in trees
dinosaurs walking with men

she says *De Vos*
never set foot in real schools but knows
that robbing them paves paths to god
hallelujahs ringing loud and vast across the land
people's money stuffed in private hands

she says *De Vos*
shoves colored kids in corners
calculates how public dollars can be raked
fed to charters and parishes and preppy enclaves
pushing god like opiates

she says *De Vos*
thumping her billionaire chest
pumping millions in proselytized promises if only
if only her vision prevails:
schools from sea to shining sea
reincarnated as vessels of christ.

she says *De Vos*
but she's *De Vorced*
her dissolution of vows cruel contortions
of constitutional mandates and laws
a zealot consumed with herself

billionaire betsy has purchased her job
unmoored unschooled unfit to lead
pimping our schools and kids to her myths
divorced from   reality   diversity   secularity
authenticity   humanity

Betsy De Vos, Trump's nominee for Secretary of Education, became the first presidential nominee to a Cabinet position in our nation's history to be confirmed only because the U.S. Vice-President cast a tie-breaking vote. De Vos came to this position with no experience in public education and with a consistent anti-public-schools track record. Once in office, she continued her militancy to use taxpayer money to fund religious and other private schools.

SCHOOL BELL

The school-child, all pudgy knees
and dimpled hands, holds close communion
with a polished beetle in the grass.

His knapsack lists on the emerald sea of dew.
Pillow fingers poke the creature, its
itinerary a graver concern to the
tardy scholar than school is.

The child's laughter tinkles in the corner of
the yard, while children scurry like lemmings
at the ringing of the bell.

Alone, entranced, the solitary
child and iridescent bug meet and confer, enwrapped
in one another's charms:
so small and at the mercy of the world,
so full of promised evolution,
compatriots oblivious to
books and clocks,
rulers and laws,
and all that bind.

NOBODY DIES

"I keep wondering why they want to kill me," Jacqueline Church Simonds,
who has coverage thanks to Obamacare, told HuffPost."
--Daniel Marans*

Promises roll out like pebbles from all their mouths, clunking and
circling their podiums at town halls, bouncing noiselessly on congress
carpet, sliding down pants legs.

How smoothly these stones swirl and roll, how satiny their circular
dances on Republican tongues, on their shoes, on their dais as they
look square in the eyes of cancer survivors and smile.

Nobody left out in the cold, sang Trump. *Nobody with rugs pulled beneath
them*, Congress crooned. *Nobody dies under our watch*, the GOP chorus
tapped and danced on TV and back home. *Nobody!*

Canes twirling, silk top hats bobbing, these comedians sing and dance
and distract with their shiny rings on fingers as they tiptoe 'round the
pebble promises and perfect cold stones underneath.

----

* In "GOP Congressman: 'Nobody Dies Because They Don't Have
Healthcare,'" *Huffington Post*, 5.6.17.

COURAGE

*"I hope that current members of Congress recall that it actually
doesn't take a lot of courage to aid those who are already powerful,
already comfortable, already influential, but it does require some courage
to champion the vulnerable and the sick and the infirm...."*
--Barack Obama*

The professor looks up from these notes, adjusts lenses on the bridge of
his nose, and takes a deep breath.

One hundred students sit silent or tap softly at their boards in the
lecture hall, risers stepping upward to the back.

The DC bubble, with its hurly-burly myths, glowers a thousand miles
hence, but here the evening sun slants through colored glass.

Vast hall hushed, the professor scans his class, exhales, and someone
says, "Exactly!"

---

* Accepting the "JFK Profiles in Courage Award," 5.7.17.

CHARLOTTESVILLE:
AUGUST 12, 2017

They were an old event unspooling itself —
lynchers and bigots rising from maggots,
crawling from basements and internet rooms
putrid with plots and misogyny.
Their hoods consigned to dust, Klansmen
reared their unmasked heads
and swooped like invading barbarians
into lovely Charlottesville.

They were an old event unspooling itself —
Nazis with armbands "heiling" the sky,
black shields emblazoned with symbols of death,
AK's and holsters, bats, pipes, and torches:
new Nazis baring teeth, spewing spit,
red faces redder beneath Tiki flames,
thundering profanities, throats raw,
in civil Charlottesville streets.

They were an old event unspooling itself —
White supremacists who've never died,
who'd just hidden themselves in prior times,
when presidents and morals muted their bullhorns,
when Supremacy trotted out its caveman dogma
mainly with others trapped with them in bubbles of steel.
Now these spider-webbed vestiges of Civil War times
brought baby-faced converts to Charlottesville streets.

No hoods, their organizers said,
only button-downs, Oxfords, khaki pants…
gotta look clean-cut and mainstream.
Gotta look legitimate, like college kids and workers,
gotta look modern, to fit in,
to appeal, expand our base,
to be relevant, win hearts and minds,
and   M!   A!   G!   A!

So baby-faced brawlers invaded the town,
unspooling their snakeskin of centuries past,
unable to modernize, unable to split
from the Klanners and Nazis and their dust of defeat.
Charlottesville women and men locked in arms,
waved signs, swung clubs, marched as one
to ward their streets, their homes, their space
against the taint of supremacist hate.

They were an old event unspooling itself—
yanks and rebs, blue and grey, north and south,
now and then, new and old, open and closed minds.
But the president took sides, even though the woman died,
and threw the killer and non-killers in the same stew,
condemning all the same, praising the "good people"
on both sides, winning praise from racists who bragged
they had handed the White House to him..

They were an old event unspooling itself —
He loves us, the Klan and Nazis assured themselves.
He didn't condemn us, they said teary-eyed,
and announced to the world: *We've only begun.*
We're not going away.
We'll spread and become the new way of life —
More and more Charlottesvilles coming your way
again and again and again.

Content based on news reports in various print and broadcast media, including *New York Times, Washington Post, Huffington Post,* CNN, NBC, and interviews in media with White nationalist leader Richard Spencer and leaders of the Unite the Right marches in Virginia.

HEATHER

Her name's Heather.
Heather Heyer.
Let her name be a rallying cry, her mother said.
Her death has magnified her.

Heather Heyer—
protestor of zealots stitched from Hitler's cloth,
of haters strapped with AK's, guns, and blades,
of disgruntleds trapped in slavery days
when they reigned supreme and trampled
on four-fifths of men.

Heather Heyer—
Sweet, sweet soul, her friends intoned,
always cleaning up her corner of the world,
tackling daily fights for color-blind rights,
skipping lunch at work
counseling grief-stricken clients,
hammering a sign on her front porch:
"Refugees welcome, for we are all one."

Heather Heyer—
voice of the voiceless, neighbors said,
sower of amity,
uncowed by Nazi arms raised as spears
against heaven.
As their boots tramped her city's streets,
their "Blood and soil!" soiling her city's air,
Heather marched for Charlottesville.

Unlike them, she bore no shield,
no clubs or pipes or bullets.
Armed only with grit and a sign,
this was, for her, another day at work:
right a wrong,
swipe an injustice away,
face down barbarians and madman steel
to fight for Charlottesville.

IDEOLOGY

*"...race is a social construct, with very little or no biological
basis. Race exists only because of racist ideologies."*
--E.E. Telles*

The Charleston 9—swathed in our tears,
Obama's heart-soothing hymn,
suffused with grace—
were barely in the ground.

Took only 2 weeks after the Last Rhodesian
to set demons loose again: fire-stoking monsters
crawling in Southern dirt at midnight
to burn what they could not squelch—

7 black churches dissolved to earth,
brick skeletons stuffed with ash and beams,
crufixes scorched like wildfire limbs,
hymnals mere charcoal skins curling under pews.

Ideology is cloth bigots fold themselves in,
melting in threads, banners and bars, souls draped on rags,
brains deadened with war myths and pseudo-gods
to justify how others are inferior.

Bigots never die, just lie low when censure strikes,
growing like worms in basements for when they can
burst, embraced, from campaign trails and internet
closets, stride to podiums, and take their nation back.

---

*In *Race in Another America*....(2004).

91

Negotiating

NEGOTIATING*

...a young mother prays

Dear God, my dearest God,
I don't know if you care about us here,
if you're in absentia, been in absentia, since November,
or if you, too, are hanging your head to clear
this shame.

I should've voted but spent time with Dave instead.
My Millie's cancer is back again,
her throat clogged, hair falling out, me tossing all night
till I cry myself asleep alongside her when
she's home.

Can't keep up, can't keep up with clinic trips,
tubes, needles in her veins, Dave grinding out two jobs,
and those politicians want to change laws,
pull the rug, take Millie's care away and stop, stop
her chance to live.

Please, please strike sense in those stubborn heads,
soften their hearts, open their eyes, let them see
the malice in their bill that kills my Millie's hope,
that dooms to death thousands more who'll be
cast aside to die.

I know I'm part to blame, my absent vote helping
him to win, him who told us he'd do this to us.
Him who counts notches on his gun like counting cash,
regardless of who's trampled in his rush
to please his base.

95

God, oh dear God, free us of this man, this stone,
and don't let him finish out his term.
Make my Millie well again, her care untouched.
Strike these politicians down with failure, till they learn
not to gamble lives!

Please, please, dear dear dear God.
No victory for *them*, only for us—
us who fight to eat, keep a roof, keep jobs—
for us who struggle and sacrifice so much
to survive.

I'll be Millie's shield, guardian, unshakeable rock,
a mother beholden to making her strong.
Just don't take her away, please don't take her away.
Let the repealers and sick-people killers drown
instead.

---

*The third stage of loss and grieving, according to Elisabeth Kubler-Ross, MD, & David Kessler's "The Five Stages of Grief," is negotiating, in which the victims of loss bargain to prevent or lessen the loss. In *On Grief and Grieving: Finding the Meaning of Grief Through the Five Stages of Loss*. (Simon & Shuster, 2005).

ART OF HIS DEALS

His life's a toilet paper roll of deals,
one, then another…endless reels
of flimsy squares that look alike.
Negotiator Don strikes
bargains that disintegrate in light
like tissue; he stretches cash so tight.

Daddy Trump saved his ass time and again,
breaking laws to give him millions when
Donald flailed and failed —
six bankruptcies and trails
of other people's broken lives,
but Negotiator always survived.

Never admit a mistake, his Dad said,
so Donald blamed others instead.
Never apologize, his father taught,
so Donald scowled, lied, and fought
like hell to cover his wrongs,
which stretch abysmally deep and long.

Never lose, Daddy Trump intoned,
so Negotiator Don honed
the art of bullying and intimidation,
which worked like a charm on our nation:
women, refugees, Mexicans, and McCain
branded as losers again and again.

His "beautiful deals" pile in rolls
of used toilet paper in bowls:
the Mexican wall, total Muslim ban,
healthcare replaced with his Trumpcare scam,
Mideast peace through his son-in-law's plan,
making coal "the king" again.

Bring back off-shored manufacturing jobs,
renegotiate NAFTA, other trade deals that rob
America from being a great nation again.
Donald promised voters that he, and only he, can
make big historic deals to make us #1,
but his flops reinforce that Don is a con.

WHY WE SUPPORT HIM

[Press Release to *Green Valley News*
Staff Reporter: September 24, 2017]

Like a therapy group or a longstanding social club, they circle their wagons at work, at the ball park, or after-hours at favorite bars.

"I don't like him," says one, sipping from his wine glass. "He's a racist and crude." He takes another drink. "But I like his tone."

He loosens his tie and takes another sip. His eyes above the rim skim the circle of six patrons—five friends and this reporter—at his table and dare anyone to disagree. His friends all nod quietly.

This is their ritual. Today it's in the San Fernando Valley at a club where guests sometimes wear cowboy boots and waitresses call everyone "Baby." But this group is a professional group: a financial advisor from Pasadena, a bank teller from the Valley, a retired business owner, and two local detectives, a man and a younger woman.

Women, men, Black, White, young, middle-aged, and a retiree. They've gelled over Trump. Nod silently at them, unbiased listener that you are at this hair-down pow-wow, open this door of communication with this group of Trump supporters, and you'll be rewarded with getting to the crux. That is this newspaper reporter's mission today.

"I've never slept as well as since Trump won," the blonde with her hair in a loosely-pinned bun sighs. She's an off-duty cop, a detective, four years on the force, and seems sure of herself, seems to speak from the heart. She gazes at the slightly older woman to her left and waits to hear what this elegantly-tailored friend, a bank teller, has to add.

"Yes, I heard all the pussy-grabbing stuff during the campaign," the teller says to nervous laughter all around. She covers her eyes momentarily, as if she's embarrassed, and tosses her long, salt-and-pepper hair over her shoulder. "But have we never heard anything like that before?"

Laughter erupts. Some men in the group shake their heads, blushing a bit. The ice is broken. This reporter shifts position, his notepad on his lap instead of on the crowded bar table.

"But cut through all the PC crap," says the male cop, gun barely visible underneath an unbuttoned white shirt now untucked. Fitting into the bar ambience more than the others in his group, he wears jeans and black, lavishly embroidered cowboy boots.

"I'm so sick and tired of PC hypocrisy," he continues after a long drink of his artisanal beer. "If I want to call a crippled man a 'cripple,' I want that freedom of speech. I don't want any schoolteacher correcting me that the new term is now..." He fishes around in his head to recollect what the PC word might currently be. "Uh, 'physically incapacitated,' or whatever the hell."

Chuckles erupt. The man next to him slaps him on the back and nods energetically.

"So," this reporter starts hesitantly, not wanting to dampen the mood of free openness that has parked itself at the table, hopefully for the duration of the interview. "So, when Trump made fun of the crippled journalist at that one rally, you know the one, when Trump mimicked him and...."

"Yeah, yeah!" the group drawls, and the blonde cop waves

her hand in a circle, as if to say, *Skip it.*

"Yeah, we remember," she mutters, nodding. "Continue."

"So you all were OK with what Trump said and did?" the reporter asks, taking a quick drink of iced water and glancing all around.

"Look," says a white-haired man who's probably in his 60's, the retired businessman. He's in a suit but he removed his tie at the beginning of the session. He rubs his hands together now, as if preparing a speech.

"Look, we don't want to curtail what the leader of the free world might say in front of cameras. That's not what we're about." He purses his lips as if closely considering how to say his next lines.

"Oh?" the reporter interrupts. "And what *are* you all about?"

"Power," blurts a beefy young man in a tight brown sweatshirt. "We want power, need power, have to have power!"

He has just sauntered over to the table from a nearby bar stool. He evidently overheard the conversation and figured out that this was some sort of a group interview involving Trump. He nods at the group at this table, smiling all around, clinks his beer bottle with the male detective, and remains standing by the group.

"Power over who, what...why?" asks the reporter, head down as he writes on his pad.

"Power is its own excuse for being," the beefy man says tritely, almost tongue-in-cheek. He looks around the table, and both detectives nod their heads and look at one another.

"Look, lives depend on having the power over someone," the blonde cop says, speaking somberly, clipping each word. "If I'm ever perceived as weak, as not having power, I'm dead." She crosses her arms and looks hard at her fellow cop. He nods, head down.

"Power determines who has a say in things," he adds. "Power determines who does what to you, and if they'll live to tell about it, or if you'll live. The President of the United States needs absolute power to spit in the face of our enemies, scare the shit out of them to keep them in line, scare the shit out of anyone here in the homeland who wants to PC the President down, scare the shit out of the pussies running the UN and taking our money for nothing. There are a lot of vultures who need a good ass-whipping to scare them straight, and Trump is *The Man* to get it done!"

The group erupts in a whoop, hands high-fiving one another. Some even rise from their chairs, clinking glasses in solidarity.

The reporter waits till the group settles itself again. "So, other than being, or seeming to be, a hard-ass you admire, was there anything Trump did or said in his campaign that enhanced your admiration of him? Or just the opposite?"

The notepad is still balanced on his lap as the reporter looks slowly around the table. A minute of silence passes while the group take drinks, look off into the distance pensively, or seem lost in thought, eyes down.

An older Black man, a sharply-dressed financial advisor, sighs and speaks in a deep, measured tone. "Look, I won't pull punches. His racism hurt. Lots of folks didn't catch it, because sometimes racism is so subtle, the speaker himself can't catch it, but Black people, young or old, have radar that picks it up as soon as racism manifests itself." He sighs again.

"What about Charlottesville?" asks the reporter.

The group seems to hold its breath.

The Black man grunts. "Brought back a lotta painful memories," he says, shaking his head slightly. "My dad marched with MLK."

The group is silent. Nobody drinks and hands are in laps.

"Those Nazis...." He doesn't finish the sentence but takes a drink instead. "I've got a lot of folks in my family history who fought the goddam Nazis in the war. They don't belong here. I wish Trump had said that...."

His voice trails off and he shrugs his shoulders. He is silent for a long, long minute.

"But who's perfect?" he says softly with a sudden smile. "Hillary had tons more baggage than that! And she's weak, crooked, wishy-washy in handling terrorists, our military, with a crook's track record that makes Trump's shenanigans look like kindergarten pranks."

Chuckles and guffaws.

"Words don't matter, man!" says the brown sweat shirt guy. "Bunch of hot air into the wind. That's all words are. Who cares if Trump said this or that about those goons in Charlottesville?"

"What's more important?" asks the retired businessman. "Words or tough actions, huh?" He looks around, but now everyone around the table is trying to get their opinions in. "Obama had lots of fancy words. Great speaker and all that. And where the hell did it get our country? Disaster!"

The blonde detective jumps in. "Those of us who know Trump's ways, who are behind him all the way, get this about him: He doesn't mean what he says," she says with each word a confident staccato. Her voice is defiant, and she glances around at the group. "He'll say whatever people at that moment, that rally

103

or whatever, want to hear. He reads us like a book and wants so hard to win the prize, so of course he'll play reality star and just throw some BS at us. We know he's blowing air, so why should we get our panties all tied up in knots?"

"Speaking as a savvy woman," the salt-and-pepper teller adds, "I couldn't care less about the Access Hollywood tape, with all the hype about sex assaults. I don't give a damn about Miss Universe, Rosie O'Donnell, Megyn, and the other dames Trump allegedly insulted. Maybe they deserved it. Maybe they started it, or maybe they just want to get big money out of him."

She looks around to gauge agreement. Her friends nod slowly, some looking down at the table, others looking at the ceiling as they sip slowly. Nobody else speaks, so she continues.

"Look, Trump is a real man, not a pretender, and he speaks rough because men can. In fact, that roughness toward females, cripples, Blacks…" [She glances tentatively at the Black man next to her] "…that roughness and lack of fear over what people would say or think must be very liberating for him, and actually for me, too, to know he has no fear and doesn't care. To me, it enhances his manly strength. He's always been a ladies' man anyway. Trump kicks ass and doesn't apologize!"

Heads nod and someone chuckles.

"His speech at 'Rocket Man Kim' from NK, threatening total destruction of North Korea, was the greatest speech I've ever heard a U.S. President make," says the beefy sweatshirt. "Torched it out of the park!" he says, tossing his head back. "Little Kim Jong Un must've been shitting nuclear bricks!"

"And frankly, I don't believe Trump wants to start a nuclear war and blow all of us up, including himself," says the retired businessman. "First off, he's not that reckless. Second, he's being the deal-maker he likes to brag about, because he *is* one! His threats about war are making all the dumb-ass leaders of Muslim-controlled Europe, with all their millions of jihadists, be scared, very scared, of Trump. Talk about bargaining power!"

The financial advisor takes a drink of wine. "Plus, he'll bring jobs back, build infrastructure...you know the plan! Hillary? Naw, Trump's the business guy who's been there, done that."

The group orders a new round of drinks. Just to be sure, this reporter asks a parting question:

"So it's mainly about tough, hard-ass, take-no-prisoners, bust those deals, scare them straight power, right?"

The reporter doesn't need to wait for an answer. The group of friends is done with his interview and is ready to party. The reporter collects his notepad and looks down at his unfinished list of questions: Russia, Colin, Paris, taxes, healthcare, hurricanes, and so many others. He sighs and finishes his glass of water.

He leaves the group of six, counting the brown sweat shirt, as they back-slap, chortle, high-five, and clink glasses with deep camaraderie and deep satisfaction.

#   #   #

COMEY
Haiku Apology

They think they know me
but can't read what's in my heart.
It's still right on course.

"Boy Scout," they've called me.
"The guy with A's in memo-
writing in college."

They said that, too,
when I produced my memos
on Trump's private talks.

I'm a hero now,
I guess. Was a villain before this--
Hillary's emails.

God, how I struggled.
Like I said: I'd throw up
if I did indeed

tip the election
for Trump. Heaven help us all!
But I meant no harm.

Loretta and Bill
didn't help with their tarmac
chat. They forced my hand.

The scales did tip,
but not just because of me.
Leaders' actions count.

Law is not fluid.
Law has stone images of
itself, carved long hence.

Stone has no heart,
and I do. But stone prevails.
Legacy beats soul.

I went to Congress
with my message hewed from stone,
but my lawman's heart.

Duty to the law,
humanity in actions
sometimes clash and slash.

This duality
confounds, topples men of rock,
but I'm human first.

My heart hurts for our
nation. I wish Trump had lost.
That's why I wrote memos.

Corruption stinks high
and is a mighty stain on
our people's freedom.

Corruption doesn't
fade with time or cleanse itself.
It soaks into souls.

I smelled it in Trump.
Lordy, I hope tapes exist,
but truth can still lose.

I've told my story
and left my trail for you.
People must persist.

'Godfathers' are sly.
Trump plays with words, always lies,
but he must.   be.   stopped.

SENATE HEALTHCARE HEARING PROTEST:
SEPTEMBER 25, 2017*

...to Sen. Hatch (R), Chairman

You sit healthy on the dais, microphone in front of you,
o powerful man, cold eyes, stone lips telling them to shut up, wishing
they disappear, silenced and whimpering back to their nursing homes,
convalescent clinics, hospices, and wherever else these twisted bodies,
deformed arms and legs, contorted figures in these goddam wheelchairs
reside.

You sit healthy on your dais, mike in front of you,
o empty man, hard lips telling Congress cops to take the old women
out, to pull them from wheelchairs like hogs, dragged by their twisted
legs, paralyzed arms, bent into pretzels despite damaged spines,
screaming and crying in pain and indignity, pleading with you and your
fellow assassins.

You sit healthy on your dais, mike in front of you,
o callous man, and watch an armless woman weep as she's dragged
outside like a pig to slaughter, still chanting as her tears flow. You stare
at the man stunted in half, chanting for mercy as he's dumped on the
floor outside your door.

You sit healthy on your dais, mike in front of you,
o rock-hearted man, and know these hundreds have waited since 5 in this
Nation's House, leaning on canes and braces, hunched
in wheelchairs, to let your death panel see their distress, so you and your
blindmen can see whom you kill.

You sit healthy on your dais for now, mike in front of you,
o robot man, minding the mindless path of your party, spouting
untruths to veneer your decrees, pandering to deep-pocket
donors and ignorant base, throwing out tattered remains of your
promises.

You sit sickly, so sickly, mike in front of you,
o cardboard man, with a hole in your chest where your heart used
to be, with eroded connections blocking your brain, with humanity
stripped and stomped on the ground, with the eyes of the world
watching you shrink.

---

*As reported by CNN and other news outlets that day, hundreds of
handicapped Americans lined up in the hall outside the U.S. Senate starting at
5 a.m. to attend Chairman Orrin Hatch's hearing on the Republicans'
proposed Obamacare repeal bill, the only hearing held prior to a Senate vote
scheduled for the following week. Only 20 handicapped people were allowed
into the hearing room, but more crowded in, desperate to be heard. The
Capitol police forcibly removed all the protestors except for the 20 allowed to
stay. Protestors were dragged from their wheelchairs with some being placed
on the stone floor. Many of the handicapped people were weeping.

A DREAMER ASKS

I know no other land but this, learned to toddle on American soil, and
rise for no other anthem but yours.
My mother wrapped me in an old, frayed towel, a round bundle in her
brown arms, and never set me down till she arrived.
From the start, she pushed English on my baby mind like she pushed
Gerber in my mouth.
Her checks from cleaning buildings light-to-night were small but
targeted like lasers on school.
Day care, pre-K, books on a rickety shelf in my room next to hers,
scuffed wood floors, little heaters plugged into the wall.

But I learned and rose, rising higher as her pride in me broke
through walls and ascended clouds.
I write, I write and write, poems and stories about her, and dad,
and how he died when I turned ten.
I grow poetic now because it's what I know: beauty in this world,
humanity she made me see,
brilliance of the human mind, freedoms of barriers smashed, things she
saw for me to make her risk her life.
I write essays for my college class, thick reports on politics and how this
nation was built on dreams,
how wave after wave of heroes and mortal gods bloomed
because of their visions of greater things.

I want to change this world as they did, to wield my American-ness for
nurturance of hope and growth,
and I've been the best, the best son, and student, the best neighbor
and friend, eyes wide and seeking truth.
So I ask you now, and every day, alongside others who traveled
in arms through desert suns and cactus nights,

other babies now grown, other toddlers pulled through thorns
and dirt many years ago, now grown,
grade-school children made to carry water in jugs, to sleep
without blankets in their dusty treks,
I ask you now why these children should be punished for their
parents' deeds,
how children without another land can be condemned to
leave their roots, now deep and strong, and let their spirits die.

MORE TEA LEAVES
...and Quandaries

      last week my cup   split in my hands
china overheated,
clumped tea leaves floating like
    tiny flotsam on the amber pool
        sliding, seeping to the table's edge
      baby puddles shimmering in lamplight
      still holding secrets

    today the cup is glazed, thick
    warrior cup
    strong to bear whatever hurts
    its belly holds
    whatever fickle plots the leaves unfold
    thick enough to cradle boiling water
    without flinching

i slowly swirl
    drops of tea leaves
      watch them spin
   and twirl
     in cliques
   hug and clump
     here
       and here
        and there
          breathe deeply
           drain the water

eyes clear and wide, alert and primed,
eyes scanning aromatic leaves,
soaked and contorted,
plumbing black-littered bottom,
searching for connections
beseeching corrections

i'd been told leaves unmask secrets
secrets read this way and that
no true path but what we think

the lightbulb overhead flickers in protest
when midnight strikes
and the leaves lie tight-lipped and cold

i'll try again next week
when i can rise for air,
when the fates will side with me,
when my heart will calm
and i'll understand.

Depression

DEPRESSION

*"When we are grieving, people may wonder about us,
and we may wonder about ourselves."*
--Elisabeth Kubler-Ross*

For three days my eyes were dry like pumice but my innards wept.
I curled like a dessicated vine in blankets twisted on my head and legs.
They said *snap out of it* but broken twigs can't move or think or feel—
dead legs, feet, hands, dead when my heart died.

When she lost, a freight train crashed into my gut. They picked me off
the carpet, smelling salts in hand. Words abandoned me for days, for
weeks, afraid to line up wrong inside my mouth, anemic, impotent, for
how could they summon what refused to show itself.

When loss is swift, when it strikes like a viper in a pot, destroying
hopes and dreams, when a mutant reigns supreme, when delusions
won the day and tossed us backward to decay, the hole that swallows
us is bottomless and vast.

Emptiness unwinds like mummy's tape, sodden and old, holding not
life but fantasies for something not proven, for something far-off and
forbidden, hidden in secrets and fear. I awoke in hollow hours each
day, for days, weeks, months. It's all I had.

Loss flattens us. My heart hurt when I pondered *her* grief, *her*
eviscerated days hiking in woods alone, deciphering how a nation let
itself be duped, how millions threw away the chance to shift cemented
views. How her heart must ache!

117

But this is how grief goes.
This is how we sink, to rise,
how brokenness is patched together again,
how despair ultimately defies death.

.

*The fourth stage of loss and grieving, according to Elisabeth Kubler-Ross, MD, & David Kessler's "The Five Stages of Grief." In *On Grief and Grieving: Finding the Meaning of Grief Through the Five Stages of Loss.* (Simon & Shuster, 2005).*

REPLAY

Press your ear on the child's chest —
he's five and in distress — his heart
fluttering like a wounded bird's,
quivering in little pearl taps you'll barely feel.

Hold his hand, just twigs chilled
and quaking, fingers in a ball so hard,
nails digging into flesh, so pull the little sticks
apart so you can place his palm in yours.

Look deeply in the child's unblinking eyes,
so wide, orbs frozen, tears layered clear,
shimmering, stopped, unflowing,
the whites like ice on coal.

Lay your ear near his mouth and hear
his rasping breath stutter like a dying man's,
uncurl his body from the kitchen floor
and hold him in your lap, hold him close, and warm.

Don't talk to him, for he won't hear.
Don't raise him up, for he won't rise.
His eyes are glued to his daddy on the rug,
the pool of red spreading dark and fast.

He's starting school next week, this little boy,
and his dad took off the day to walk him there.
Uncurled, sitting in your lap, his head
tilted to his father, the child's in distress.

Don't speak to him, for he can't hear.
Don't stand him up, for he can't stand.
His pencil legs quiver on yours, his silent lips
wet now because his tears unplugged themselves.

In the other corner, on the floor, the cop bawls
like a man condemned, his pistol on the chair,
his red face bobbing in his trembling hands,
as clueless now as when his holster freed his gun.

Tonight the screens will flash the dead man
in his uniform, and tell how he went deaf
in war, and how he saw his window break and summoned
help, and how all hell broke loose.

AIR SHOW: CHICAGO
AUGUST 2017

sun's skinny fingers puncture gray clouds,
jets slice sky in thunder,
scream past treetops, rattle bones.

on my back porch, i ladle soil with my mother's scoop,
tole tin handle faded and bent,
seedlings standing steady in shade.

with leather gloves and a copper spade,
i mound loam 'round gentle juniper roots,
filling grandmother's jardinière.

half-mile away, trios of jets slope upward,
determined arcs deafening,
syncopated swoops splitting the vast.

crowds love this, my neighbor says,
holding his daughter's small-flag hand,
hurrying past my porch for a primo spot.

i imagine uptilted heads by lake michigan,
mouths agape with gasp and awe,
children perched on father shoulders.

the watchers' trembles aren't for fear
on chicago grass, blankets, picnic treats spread lush.
they know this is just a show.

but these same jets scream over trees
on the other side, over desert towns,
over blasted roofs, over bodies crushed by stone.

these midnight jets boom across oceans,
rain fire on villages, mountains, skyscrapers like ours,
mosques flattened to dust.

their village children hold no flags.
their elders run from doorways, hunched in fear.
these jets' booms explode their chests.

i sweep cuttings from my porch,
set freshly potted plants on rattan tables by my door,
drink iced tea in my padded chair.

jets roar for an hour more,
but i know their thunder overseas will never cease.
for this—for *this*—i tremble.

BY THE L·A· FREEWAY

1

Young black man, shirt stretched tight across his
shoulders, muscles undulating, lanky legs moving
suavely from car to car as he leans toward the glass,

offers anemic bouquets to drivers at the light, by
the ramp, who tap fingers at the sight of backed-up
cars on the concrete headache just above.

Too young to be freeloading, they say. Young
black man's white-teeth smile is supple, a band of light across
his dark. Too young, too healthy for sympathy, they
say and turn away. Should be throwing footballs at
the high school or the park,

should be throwing out his cardboard sign, grimy
hand-scrawled bit of corrugated crap that lies: "Please
help a vet. Hungry, sick."

He taps his black finger on rolled up windows, flashes his only
whiteness, smiles with lips pressed tight when driver after
driver at the light looks away and pretends he isn't there.

2

Young black man, prickly blanket spread between two
cans, lanky legs tucked beneath old sheets layered
on for warmth, candle in tuna tin shimmying near his arm,

123

offers bottle to the khaki man in sleeping bag,
his nighttime meal on a piece of rag pinned down with
stones as he fumbles in his pocket for a spoon.

Young black man's smile lies dark. Too young,
they'd said, too young to go, to fight, too young
to die so far away. Should be throwing footballs in
the college down the road instead. Sympathy wasted on
him then, absent now since who knows when.

His hand-scrawled sign lies face-up in a puddle
near his head. He coils his blanket like a jelly roll,
discipline remembered. Young black man vomits out his soul,

rubs his fingers on closed eyes, blotting out the day, the red
desert nights, rattles and shouts, then prays with lips pressed
tight, pretending he was never there.

AT ALL COSTS

*"People only cheat you when they can't
beat you in a fair fight."*
—Rev. William Barber

The man who lives in towers always played this way,
Taught well by his father, as he himself was.
Being second is being broken, beaten to a puddle of spit.
Being last is the last toehold to hell.
Don't call yourself the greatest if you're not at the top.

If you can't win, win ugly.
If you can't win, win dirty and sodden in stench.
But win.

If you can't beat them, smear them.
If you can't beat them, kick them in the spine.
But beat them.

If you can't beat them, cheat them.
Gather round snakes that charm with deadly tongue,
That hypnotize with lies and lures that shine.

Stack up men with crooked thumbs,
With microphones wired to dens of thugs,
Grime-coated keyboards clacking with myths.

If you can't beat them, cheat them.
Slide in the KG's from dark-shade enclaves,
Rubles in trench coats and diplomats' rooms.

Send out your billionaire cronies at dusk
Through backdoors, back-channels created for you,
Meetings in towers, translators in tow.

If you can't beat them, cheat them.
Black men, brown men with ballots in hand
Shoo-ed away empty, names ghosted from rolls.

Cheat big and broad, with piles of conspirators
Eager for podiums, big bucks, and thrones.
Losers hogtie themselves with scruples and rules,
But winners go bold, jump laws, and innovate.
Cheaters always win.

WHEN OUR HOUSES TALK

"Make yourself comfortable," said the window treatments
as they closed themselves on a sunny day.
--Advertisement, Hunter Douglas shades*

Smart, intelligent shades simplify your life, the Madison Men go on to say, and brag how these shades move themselves through the day so you won't have to. Won't have to move, or think, or fight with that satan sun while you're swishing cubes in bourbon.

"Sleep tight, everyone," said the window treatments as they lowered themselves for the night — another: in *House Beautiful*. Sleep tight in your Tempurpedic, swathed in French Yves Delorme down, in silk PJ's, the two of you, your platinum watches on Henredon nightstands.

Cross-town, houses weep as they speak.

Sleep tight, the bunk bed sighs at three twig-legged sisters spooned in grandma's quilt. *Sleep tight,* cement floor mutters at grizzled men on cardboard in a demolished house.

Be comfortable, moan walls to 13 Salvadorans in a 2-room tenement in East LA, sun lashing the lone cracked window. *Make yourself comfortable,* and don't mind the sun, since your day is done, whisper floorboards while doorways look away.

Sleep tight, a barred window murmurs at a bruised mother with toddlers trembling under cots nearby. *Make yourself comfortable,* the basement bulb says, its light shimmying on puddles by their broken sink.

Hunter Douglas houses coo and swish and soothe, sweetness oozing from every slat, every fold, every silken drape as their magic words pamper owners to sleep and rest.

Cross-town houses weep life.

---

* In *Traditional Home* & other upscale home décor magazines, 2016, 2017.

MANICURE DIVA:
HONG HANH, APRICOT BLOSSOM

When they call her "diva," she ducks her head, her thick
        hair falling like curtains to shield her cheeks.
She looks up only to greet clients or reach for tools she
        wields with grace and skill unmatched in the
        salon.

*Hong Hanh: manicurist extraordinaire, epitome of modesty and
        expertise*! her clients rave.
They heap praise upon their diva, petite lady of amber eyes
        and perfect teeth, artist who cuts and trims and
        swooshes and colors and transforms the mundane
        to majestic.
They dip into Calvin Klein and Kate Spade bags for tips to
        stuff into Hong's flowered pockets or press into her
        hand.

But when doors are locked, and
Americans are gone, and
lamplight paints the sidewalks yellow, and
tall glass windows turn black and cold, and
Hong flips the OPEN sign around, and
sweeps the floor in urgent arcs,

a pall hangs in the shop. Specters float beside her at the sink, as
she rinses scissors and clippers and fruit for the shrine behind the
counter.

Hong Hanh: tiny woman of Saigon fields, of brothers slain in
wars and sisters enslaved in beds.
Hong Hanh: aborter of two children from rapist monsters.
Hong Hanh: daughter of parents abandoned in a land lost in mist
and misery.

Her hands work magic by day, and pray by night.
Her head bows over hands by day, and bows on the ground by
        night, tears staining photos and rugs and wooden floor.
Her heart lies calm and meek in the salon by day, and flails with
        grief by night,
        each night,
her escape across oceans to freedom unable to free her soul.

CRUELEST MAN

*"The most ignorant, cruelest, most narcissistic and inhumane man
to ever sit in the Oval Office is in charge of the armed forces, FEMA
and the nuclear codes."*
--Jennifer Rabin, "The Saddest Day of This Administration."

The man who tweets and golfs *ad infinitum*
condemned an island nation to death—
    3 million human beings,
    10th day of their hurricane disaster,
    10th day of starvation, illness, dehydration, fear,
death "in a war zone," our general said on the scene.

In bilious tweet taps* as he lolled in his millionaire club, strutted
importantly across golf greens, outed his hatred
of brown and black skin, and
sneered his contempt of women with rank,
the narcissist
condemned Americans to death.

No U.S. troops to clear roads.
None dispensing supplies across ravaged towns.
None binding broken bodies
as American soldiers can.
Absentee slumlord fiddled, drank wine, ate caviar
while the woman he trashed in his tweets
trudged daily in sewage and sludge
to save American lives.

For how can relievers span "vast oceans"
to an island blot on the map
severed from hard ground where the narcissist
must take time off to golf when duty wears him out.
And why should America help Puerto Rico,
that "far, far away" alien land where
slackers can't fend for themselves.

This is the man, yes, this is the man
with fingers near nuclear codes, the man
who can order a nation be bombed,
send planes, boots, submarines and ships,
wherever on earth he wants...
but not to P.R. to save American lives —
this *"most ignorant, cruelest, most narcissistic and inhumane"*
occupant of our People's House.

---

* Published in *Huffington Post*, 9.30.17. Trump's tweet, sent from his luxurious New Jersey golf resort on a vacation which was paid for by the American people, was this: *"Such poor leadership ability by the Mayor of San Juan and others in Puerto Rico, who are not able to get their workers to help. They want everything to be done for them when it should be a community effort."*

The mayor of San Juan, the Puerto Rican capital, Carmen Yulín Cruz, is a respected bilingual Latina who, throughout the hurricane disaster, slept on a cot, spent days looking for survivors to rescue, often wading in hip-high sewage and toxic waters, and helped dispense supplies to survivors as best she could. The people, as shown on TV, at the time Trump tweeted the comment above, and continuing throughout the hurricane's aftermath, worked hard to clear the debris, salvage their remaining possessions, repair their homes, and help one another.

On television, the mayor wept as she begged Trump and anyone else listening to help Puerto Rico, to send drinking water and save lives. Trump's tweet came the day after this plea. At that time, Trump had not set foot on Puerto Rico to view the damage and console the people, as he had readily done in Texas and Florida.

DREAMER WITH BRAIDS

Like docile snakes, your braids lie thick,
blackness glossy and knotted to your waist. Your
tendril beard and sideburns shock
when you raise your face
and show the world that you're a man:

poet man, brown poet from Maya-land, glorified
in rhyme stilted with accents raw, words
that stumble on furling tongue, that catch
sometimes to tell the world you came from
jungles misted in centuries of mystery and loss.

Brown poet with braids, caramel fingers
slender on pencil songs, soul enwrapped in
other times, pyramid stones, and blood
curling its way down massive steps
where giants worshipped sun and death.

Brown poet man, gentle snakes on back,
face intent in this new land, dreams binding
distant lores and newfound shores, eyes seeing
things unseen by fathers buried deep —
new poems in cloth-bound books, and hope.

PASTOR JEDIDIAH

"I see lives being destroyed, and I don't know what to do....
I lay in my bed and my heart beats so heavy for the city,
that it drives me to tears."
—Jedidiah Brown*

Chosen one at the storefront church on a street where bodies pile in
alleys and empty lots,
daily death, weekly carnage in Chicago, the South Side redder and
meaner than drug dealer dens.
Your roots, Jedidiah: blocks and hoods engraved in your brain, your
soul, for these are your childhood friends, first loves and all.

Chosen one, picked when you were twig-legged, just a manchild with
13 years and another name,
the old woman prophet drawing you aside, sent by God to tell you—
you just a poor Black kid with Bibles—to tell you God marked you for
his work.

Like the fisher of men, you cast wide nets to sweep homeless into your
home, beaten mothers, and runaways with spirits long snuffed.
You ministered with love more than Bibles, fed, mentored, struggled to
make them feel human again.

Chosen one who forgot to take care of yourself—
outsize dreams born of firsthand pain, warrior heart girded
to bind daily loss, to soothe armies of demons devouring your town.
When you salve wounds, quench fires and give hope to people looking
for peace,
there's not enough of you to go around.

134

You've set down the gun pressed to your temple, silenced sobs that
wracked you when you drove to the lake.
We all heard you, Jedidiah, heard you clear that heavy day, heard your
heartbreak
weeping for your failures to save lives.
We saw crowds 'round your car, police begging you, some on their
knees, some sobbing,
for they knew you, Jedidiah,
your vigils on burning streets, bullhorn and open hands.

How hard justice is to find, peace to pin down, love to spread!
How hard it is, how hard, to fight day and night,
to slice open our heart to wounds of our brothers,
to rise with the sun, day after day, when others are flat on the ground.

---

*"And So Jedidiah Brown Gave All of Himself to the City He Loved: A New
Generation of Black Leaders Confronts the Anguish of Activism," by Ben
Austen. In *Highline: Huffington Post*, 9.28.17.

Acceptance

ACCEPTANCE*

There comes the day. It always does.
In time, through bits and pieces of acceptance,
we realize the past can't be maintained intact,
Elisabeth says.

The new status quo prevails,
as we grit our teeth,
gird our loins,
and soldier on however we must.
Our lives are significantly changed.
But, Elisabeth tells us, *it's time to heal.*

Our nation picks up scattered puzzle shards
from the daily detritus of Trump.
Piecing the breakage together again
may take wizards, shamans,
crystal ball gazers,
tea leaf readers divining tomorrows,
but the journey of loss has been walked.

All roads face forward from here.

---

*The fifth and final stage of loss is acceptance, which does not mean
happiness or agreement with what is now status quo.

CHILDREN ASK

I.

Is it true, Mr. President, you're an immigrant??

Did your mom spend time with you, Mr. Trump? Did she kiss you, hug you, sing to you?

I know your daddy was rich, but did you get an allowance? Did you have to work for it?

Did your father always tell you he loved you? (Do *you* love *your* sons the same way?)

Who taught you manners?

Did anyone or anything make you afraid or very sad?

Were you bullied when you were little? Did kids ever make fun of you, or punch you?

Did you ever cheat in school? Like on big tests or little quizzes? Or homework? (Even just a little bit?)

Is it true you don't like science and reading? But why?

Is this *TRUE*, Mr. Pres.?? ? You punched your teacher in second grade??!!

II.

Who was the "big love" of your life—in adolescence, young adulthood, or beyond? Have to ask this, 'cause you've had 3 wives, & tons of kids & grandkids. Just wondering.

Is love more important to you than fame? Success? Power? Or...? (We get asked this in HS all the time, as if it matters.)

Who do you consider "American"? Who is more of a "real American": Koch Bros., Joe Arpaio, or Barack Obama?

How can I support you, like my family does, and stay true to my humanitarian tendencies (Homeless Rescue Mission, Rotary Club, LGBTQ civil rights, etc.)? Help!

Why do you love Putin so much? (U chose him over all leaders at European summit and always defend him — stunning!)

Why do you "hate losers"? Have you never, ever, ever failed??!

Is it true that loyalty is #1 with you? Can't put down KKK, Nazis or White Supremacists, but you trash media, BLM, etc. like nothing. If someone's loyal to you, they're OK?

Can you stick to a position on any issue for more than a day without changing your mind and tweeting about it? (Name a political stance you've never deviated from.)

For my Social Studies report, Mr. Trump: What have you *personally* (not your foundation) done to help poor people or vulnerable folks...without pay, fanfare, photo ops, politics, or any publicity (you know, rolling up your sleeves, making direct personal contact...you get the picture).

See if you can handle this one, Mr. 45 — Why do people lie, and why do some people lie so much!...why do you?

MELANIA, OH MELANIA

My heart hurts when I see you on TV,
elegant, regal, quiet,
a little island in Trumpworld,
a spot of seeming gentility in perfect-storm waves.
Hands hanging straight, model pose,
fingers slightly curled, not relaxed or afraid,
head high although, in others,
it might hang as a beaten prisoner's face.

My heart hurt for you when I saw you on TV,
rail-spike heels sinking in earth,
you leaning into rain and wind,
heading for the plane where there's no place to hide
from him.
Were your slippers in your bag?
Warm, enveloping, meant for your own comfort,
not his.

How many tears have left your guarded eyes
in dusky tower rooms away from him,
his scowl and razor words soiling screens
downstairs, in the bar,
where people can't forget
he sleeps with you
and your beloved Barron is
his flesh and blood.

BARRON

lanky for your age, perfectly suited in white shirt
and tie, gentle blonde hair and angel face, the sweet
delight of your mother's eyes

like her, we love you, Barron, for no child should
bear slings and arrows meant for a man, no child should weep
or fear beneath the burden of name

lonely bird in gold-plated cage, ninth floor of opulence in
marbled tower, toys and books, precocious talks with
mother in the bond she carefully molded with you

we love you, too, Barron, your brilliant child's mind, your
quietness in pews, amidst pomp and circumstance, in White
House halls when you appear, head down, face still

guarded like pharoah's treasure, world prize for
ransommers, a parent's nightmare, and you imprisoned
guiltless in fortune and fame

our nightmare, too, for no child should feel burdens of
walls and threats, no child should be bereft
of running free in meadows open and blue

we see you, Barron, your radiant innocence, as
your father flails, and those rare times you smile, we want
to wrap you in accepting arms

TRUMP'S P.R. TWEETS:
10/1/17

Trump was a busy man, tweeting for days
about Black athletes with knees on grass:
23 tweets condemning
S.O.B.'s dishonoring country & flag.

7 proclaiming faux concern
for Brown and Black people
in Puerto Rico
still dying of thirst,
starvation,
and disease.

DARK-MUSTACHIOED MAN

The dreamy, dark-mustachioed man
seemed a sculpture, his Valentino face chiseled
and somber in the shadow of potted palms where
the bistro walls met. He might have been in
silver-studded velvet astride a stallion, reins
firmly in hand, sweeping a Marquesa into
his arms, fleeing the hacienda for their
nightly tryst under the sultry moon.

But he moved, broke his pose.
The dark-mustachioed man
strode to a vacated table,
wiped it clean in three swift strokes,
then shrugged, wet rag in hand,
"I no speak English,"
when a bristle-faced patron in a dirty red cap,
large sweat stains under his armpits,
asked him where the men's room was,
then grunted at the ignorance of Meskins.

13 DAYS:
MR. TRUMP GOES TO PUERTO RICO

13 days after Maria's four-star assault on an island belonging to us,
13 days after paradise was lost,
13 days after P.R. wept onscreen and begged us for aid,
13 days and 34 deaths

endless days past Mr. Trump's apoplexy with athletes and owners he
couldn't control,
countless days past Mr. Trump's wining, dining, golfing, and whining,

Mr. Trump crossed 'big ocean' to land on 'the island, it's an island
surrounded by water!'
as he in his pre-visit wisdom intoned.

Mr. Trump went to Puerto Rico today, without MAGA cap, without
merchandise,
Melania at his side without spikes.

My people at FEMA are great!
I have an A+ for the great work I've done on disasters.
Everyone raves about me and my aid.

Mr. Trump went to Puerto Rico today, without John Kelly holding his
leash,
without teleprompters to keep him in line.

Puerto Rico should be glad only 16 people died.
Thousands died at Katrina, a real catastrophe!
Helping you has thrown our budget a little out of whack.

Mr. Trump went to Puerto Rico today, a quick trip to sit with officials
and chat,
have photo ops, throw towels, and self-aggrandize.

It's now acknowledged what a great job we've done.
Your governor has given us the highest praise.
We have done a great job with an impossible situation!

A cursory drive past demolished homes and trees lying legs-up,
a few handshakes,
and Trump was done.

Trump's comments made in Puerto Rico, shown in italics above, are direct
quotes or paraphrases from online news reports in *IntelligencerPost, The New York
Times,* and on *CBSNews* on October 3, 2017, the date of Trump's first post-
hurricane visit to the island.

SOMETIMES

…we just need to
clear our heads, shake
them hard with eyes on clouds and wisps that float
to corners of heaven

eyes on golden slants that light up curled
edges of gingko tree leaves, tiny
spotlights teasing sparrows on high wires

sometimes we just need to
keep eyes up, above treetops, beyond
cumulus parked on mountains
as far as our heads can tilt

keep eyes soft when we lie on
grass, to see the infinite blue of humanity's
roof, the ocean birthed first

sometimes we just need to
elevate eyes to air, wind, ether, weightless
realm of eagles, lightness and
all that is good

MAYOR CARMEN

"When it bothers someone that you're asking for drinking water,
medicine for the sick and food for the hungry, that person has much
deeper problems than what can be discussed in an interview."
--Carmen Yulín Cruz*

He called her "nasty woman," so she wore "NASTY" like a medal on
her T-shirt on TV.
He called her a bad leader, so she focuses like hell's laser on saving her
people's lives despite him.

He thinks he can tweet her into silence, degrade her into turnabout.
She's a Latina after all, poor, homeless, with a heart that feels every cut
the broken branches make on her people's hands when they clear
roads.
She feels every parched breath pushed like knives into old people's
throats in a nursing home when generators sighed and died.
She feels brittle bones of people she helps pull from waters toxic and
putrid.
She feels men's pain when they cart sisters and mothers and fathers
from splintered homes sodden and deadly.
She feels the abyss of grief when she sees toddlers and children
muddied and still.
She feels the rumbles and stabbings of hunger and thirst of people
stranded alone.

Mayor Carmen wears glasses, rubber waders thick and heavy to her
hips, wears her outrage and pleas on her face and lips like Melania
wears de la Renta with heels.

Mayor Carmen knows no vanity, like him and her.
Mayor Carmen knows no rest, like him and her in their resort when he
lambasted her.

Mayor Carmen knows death and fear, desperation and tribulation,
isolation and abandonment every day that breaks.
We don't have time for her political noise, Trump's team says.
Mayor Carmen knows he doesn't care.

It's not politics, she said to him.
We need water, she said on TV for the thousandth time with the death
toll 39.

But for him it always is,
and they'll have water when he gets around to it.

---

* The mayor of San Juan, the capital of Puerto Rico and its largest city, is Carmen Yulín Cruz. Three weeks into the natural disaster, she asked again on TV for drinking water for her nation. The Director of FEMA, Brock Long, replied: "We filtered out the mayor a long time ago. We don't have time for the political noise." [Interview on "ABC News This Week," 10.8.17]

LETTER OF FORGIVENESS

...It's Never Too Late

October 28, 2017

Dear President Trump:

We are the American Coalition of Nonsectarian Pastors for Peace (AC-NPP), based in your childhood borough of Queens in New York City. As the National President of this large group, and as a former Presbyterian, as is your own religious affiliation, I write to you now with a heart heavy with sadness but uplifted with hope.

Your young presidency, nearing the one-year milestone, has suffered controversies and denigrations that would tear apart any President's heart, or any pastor's spirit. Our Coalition has followed closely the challenges your presidency has faced, has discussed these, and has reflected extensively upon remediations to assuage your own embattled situation and the hurts of this great nation.

In short, we believe you and our nation—*all or mostly all the people of this country*—can flourish in a win-win situation for America. Thank you for giving some of your time and attention to our proposals for bringing Americans together under your leadership. To wit:

- *Mr. President, please lay your campaign to rest.*
  Breaking from the past rhetoric is uppermost. You are now President of not just your base, and not *mostly* your base, but of all the people, the majority of whom did not vote for you, sir. So rallies with your base, with your slogans from the past, your "promises" from the past, need to be set aside in order to move forward, no matter how difficult this may be for you.

- *Please read and learn what the majority of Americans want for our/their nation.*

  It is clear that the "promises" you made in your campaign are not reflective of what most Americans need and want today. When you campaigned, public sentiment toward "Obamacare," for example, may have justified your position on it. But not anymore. With the passage of time and with Americans learning more about what a healthcare repeal will cause, losing Obamacare is now one of the greatest fears facing the majority of our people, even many of your voters. Finding facts to guide you is not difficult, Mr. President. Even though national polls differ among themselves, certain trends and conclusions are clear to identify. Some of these needs and wishes of the American people are listed below.

- *As almost all U.S. Presidents have had to do once in office, please modify your campaign agenda to reflect the changing political landscape vis-à-vis the needs and strong wishes of the American majority.*

  The majority of our nation does not want a wall; a Muslim ban; the dismantling and termination of environmental protections; denial of climate science; a return to coal; removal of women's reproductive rights; voter suppression; denial of equality to LGBQT human beings; nuclear proliferation; expansion of the military; or the possibility of war. It is the *minority of the people* who may want these for our nation. Are you the "minority President," sir? Or are you leader of all?

- *Please break with racial ideologues whose words, writings, and actions dehumanize, demonize, and disenfranchise ethnic and racial minorities, in effect stripping them of their humanity.*

  Nothing but total rejection of white supremacy in any form or shape will heal our nation. (Their names and labels don't matter;

their ideology does.) This may also enhance your chance to win hearts and minds of your resistors, for they are right, and they will never stop fighting you on racism, or your perceived racism.

- *Please embrace diversity, for it is the common denominator across our world now.*

    A fight to save what is obsolescent is futile and is part of the reason protestors defy your presidency. America will no longer be ruled by "the majority race" exclusively as time marches forward. In addition, women will be increasingly irrepressible, as they should be, comprising half of our nation and of the world. America has the most productive workforce on earth, and our economy is the largest. Our workforce comes in all colors, backgrounds, and origins. Embrace this and regularly express your respect of and appreciation for the multicultural, multi-gender fabric of our society. Actions speak louder than words, Mr. President. Why not fill your Cabinet, your advisor teams, with many more women and with people of color?

- *Please stop the deconstruction of our government.*

    As a complex, large country, we need more experts to handle the "work of the people," which is your number one priority, sir: the people. Not corporations, lobbies, radical ideologues, billionaires or millionaires, but the *everyday American people*. When our governmental infrastructure is stripped to its girders, with agencies understaffed, labs and research groups terminated, diplomats removed from around the world (especially in "hot spots"), White House offices and resources left empty, and social services support systems stripped and allowed to die, *the people suffer*. Trimming waste is one thing, sir. Amputating vital limbs and organs is another.

- *Divest, and please send your family home.*

  The latest national poll has revealed a troubling concern, for the first time in our nation's history: the #1 fear of the American people is *corruption in our government.* The majority of Americans believe that their President is financially aggrandizing himself and his family via the presidency. Terrorism is no longer our greatest fear. Americans are most concerned that your administration, sir, has opened the door to corruption in our democracy, via nepotism and the large number of billionaires with questionable histories that you have brought into the White House, something no other American President has done.

- *Please surround yourself with experts in the field, each field.*

  Not loyalists. Not extremists. Not those intent on deconstructing our democracy. Not people whose personal enrichment and coddling, at taxpayers' expense, is prime. Not unvetted people whose backgrounds hold troubling secrets or inconsistencies. Not people whose personal, financial, and/or ideological agenda throughout their careers have been the opposite of what they are charged with managing *for the well-being of the majority of the American people.*

∞∞

Our dear President, please pardon our audacity in writing these words to you. We hold little power, no influence in the world at large. But we care deeply about our democracy, about the prosperity and health of our nation and all its people. We care deeply about your success, for your success in allowing all the people of our nation to flourish in peace and confidence translates to America's profound success and to the enduring strength of our democracy.

None amongst us is infallible, and the best we can do as we turn a page for redemption or reinvention is to ask for forgiveness for any misdirection we inadvertently or erroneously pursued, for any omission in which we unwittingly or wittingly engaged. Owning our misspoken words and our untoward actions regarding others is the hallmark of all great leaders, and it helps societies prosper.

We pray in solidarity that our offer of support and assistance will be well-met by you and those on whom you rely for your effective leadership. We stand ready to meet with you to discuss how our participation and contributions might serve you and our nation. The attached sheet contains the signatures of 6,187 of our member pastors throughout our country. We are all brothers in our commitment to making our nation responsive to the needs and wishes of *all* those whom our government rules and serves.

Yours in peace and hope,

William Marconi Porter

William Marconi Porter
National President
American Coalition of Nonsectarian Pastors for Peace

MOTHER'S DAY REMEMBRANCE

each treasure that surrounds me is one you lacked:
peaceful mornings, birds singing me awake
the warmth of sunlight slanting on my quilt
backyard benches in swaying gingko shade
lantana, lavender, orchids, and irises
coffee cups and memories
first thing each day
in my garden

this day, mother's day
I sit quiet in morning mist and noonday sun
connected still to earth, sky, cloud,
to balms of nature that sit with me each breath
nature's bounty—my companion—
as i remember you

i miss you here
you lived among thorns, burrs, stones, and mud
with dandelions and milkweed for gardens
bore deprivations born of bigotry
saw family carted back across border walls
back to satan suns and frozen dirt
without respite from harshness
or beauty for balm

i miss you here
among hummingbirds and bees, beside bonsai trees
sitting with me in the gentle world you dreamed
i miss you here
i miss you here

THIS I KNOW

the man at the head is not the
    head beautiful women have calloused
        hands the blind cannot forget what they've
    seen the deaf hear us loud and clear children
    lead the world priests and pastors mullahs
and rabbis are empty insanity is truth and
        truth is insane

we seek formulas and maps to shape our
    humanity squander eyes bury voice squelch
instinct and know more about facebook videos screens
        texts cars clothes cocktails malls and
    superficial things that distract derail mislead to
take us off the road the frontier is inside

and misunderstood forgotten blended in with
lands we navigate thinking this is the territory to
        explore and learn and we're off
        the road and blind and deaf and dumb until
        years piled in corners to the rafters help us peel
away layer by layer trivialities that sidelined wisdom and
        humanity that made us reach this point not
    knowing still not
        knowing what it's all about

HILLARY AFTERWARD

*"There are times when all I want to do is scream into a pillow....
I felt that I had let everyone down. Because I had."*
--Hillary Clinton*

Losing with victory at my fingertips
hit hardest.

Conceding to a cheat stabbed deep, for the
con was huge.

Facing loss, in lonely hikes in misty woods,
had grief in every breath.

Not winning for my mother and daughter and women worldwide,
   not reading my victory speech to them,
      not being in the People's House battling for them,
         decimated my spirit as no enemies could.

Rising from ash is brutal when you feel hollowed out
and counted gone.

But my gut is still steel, my spine iron, my mind forged in flame,
and I will never quit.

---

*"Annals of Politics: Still Here. Hillary Clinton looks back in anger," by David Remnick. *The New Yorker*, 9.25.17.

2020

have you foreseen the decade 'round the corner,
looming with teeth fully bared,
partisans lined in gauntlets
with elephant memories of grievances deep,
guttural throats
growling reminders
of sick people crying in congressional halls,
of brown people dying in paradise lost

on the other side of the divide,
hoodless men with leather straps on chests,
with shields not board but military-grade,
boots of steel tramping city streets,
german cries with arms to skies,
plots to ram not once
but blocks and blocks and blocks
of protest signs

READING TEA LEAVES AFTER TRUMP

Tea leaf messages are clearer
with time, they say.
One hundred cups and more
I've gazed into the wet, the dark, the clumps
of unnamed words, notes,
missives of the undisclosed.

A pinch of leaves,
mere fragments of the parent plant,
baby pieces tasked with telling tales,
curling, stretching for 3 minutes in boiled water,
giving me the chance to understand.

I've drunk deep,
heat cauterizing vocal chords,
sanitizing ignorance
to insure what I interpret is correct.

My gaze impales dots and swirls
at the bottom of my china cup,
but long ago I learned the sloping sides
and whiteness don't grant wisdom.

In this era of not knowing,
of chaos and dissembling,
of alternative facts and fakes galore,
of conventions displaced with crudeness,
of free speech allowed for friends not foes,
of voters cocooned in clueless complacence,
of a leader devoid of leadership genes,

truth slams me like a cudgel,
strips me of vague eyesight that once gave guidance
in the other days,

the days before,

forcing me to understand
not tea leaves,
no, not tea leaves,
but to understand
that not knowing
is all
we'll know
after Trump.

About the Author

Photo by Victor A. Reyna

Thelma T. Reyna is the multiple-national-award-winning author of four books—a short story collection, two poetry chapbooks, and a full-length collection of her poems—as well as editor of two poetry anthologies, each comprising over 100 poems by Southern California writers. Her short fiction, poetry, and nonfiction have been published in books, literary journals, textbooks, anthologies, magazines, and other print and online media for over 25 years.

Reyna is founder, owner, and Chief Editor at The Writing Pros consultancy. She was Poet Laureate in Altadena, CA in 2014-2016. She holds a Ph.D. from UCLA.

www.GoldenFoothillsPress.com

Acknowledgments

The following poems were originally published in a prior version in the publications noted below:

- "This." *Spectrum Anthology, #5.* (Spectrum Publishing, ed. Don Kingfisher Campbell).
- "New." *2016 San Gabriel Valley Poetry Calendar.* (Palabra Productions, ed. Don Kingfisher Campbell).
- "Inaugural: Haiku Sequence." *Lummox Anthology, #6, 2017.* (Lummox Press, ed. RD Armstrong).
- "Kellyanne." *Spectrum Anthology, #12: Poets for Change.*
- "Shadow Love" [originally titled "Wrong Love"). *2011 Emerging Urban Poets.* (Palabra Productions, ed. Don Kingfisher Campbell).
- "Hunger." *Rising, Falling, All of Us,* by Thelma T. Reyna (Golden Foothills Press, 2014).
- "School Bell." *San Gabriel Valley Poets Quarterly,* Summer 2011 (Palabra Productions, ed. Don Kingfisher Campbell).
- "Ideology." *San Gabriel Valley Poets Quarterly,* Fall 2015.
- "By the L.A. Freeway." *Caper Literary Journal* [online journal], ed. Lisa Marie Basile. August 4, 2010.
- "Manicure Diva: Hong Hanh, Apricot Blossom." *San Gabriel Valley Poets Quarterly,* Winter 2012.
- "Dreamer with Braids" [originally titled "Poet with Braids"]. *Hearts in Common,* by Thelma T. Reyna (Finishing Line Press, 2013).
- "Dark-Mustachioed Man." *Rising, Falling, All of Us.*
- "When Our Houses Talk." *Spectrum Anthology, #4: 2016 Top Ten San Gabriel Valley Poets.*
- "This I Know." *Hearts in Common.*

NOTE: All writings attributed with specific names to others (e.g., haiku, memo, letters) are the authors' original creations, representing fictionalized personas. All tweets are Thelma T. Reyna's creations written in the spirit of actual tweets posted by the people depicted.

**National Award-Winning
Literary Book Press:**

*Over 100 authors published
in Southern California*

Our indie-published books have won a total of 14 national book honors. Visit our website to see our poetry collections and new novel at www.GoldenFoothillsPress.com

Author **Thelma T. Reyna** is available for literary events, book signings, classroom presentations in high school and college, book clubs, panel presentations, and as a guest speaker or workshop presenter on varied topics.

Contact her at:
www.GoldenFoothillsPress.com
goldenfoothillspress@ yahoo.com

Page for Notes

Page for Notes